Accession no
36227~~

D1189212

All Business is Local

LIS - LIBRARY

Date	Fund
20/04/16	xe-Shr

Order No.	
2705977	

| University of Chester | |

Introduction:

THE PERSISTENCE OF PLACE

Real Madrid brings in more revenue than any other soccer club worldwide—topping the list in 2010 for its fifth consecutive year.[1] Rabid Spanish soccer fans undoubtedly contribute to this success, but they comprise only one element of the story. Real Madrid was among the first soccer clubs in the world to recognize the power of global marketing—recruiting players of different nationalities to supplement the team's Spanish core and bolster its global brand. It deploys its increasingly popular Web site, www.realmadrid.com, along with social media like Facebook, Twitter, and YouTube, to provide content in Spanish, English, Japanese, and Arabic, and interact with fans all over the world. Official merchandise, which along with licensing fees, accounts for about one third of annual revenue, is sold both online and in more than ninety countries. For the 2009–2010 season, the club reported that overseas sales of the cobranded Adidas-Real merchandise "substantially surpassed sales at a national level."[2]

Real Madrid is clearly a global brand. At the same time, there is no doubt that a large part of its appeal comes from its association with the city of Madrid itself. It may seem at odds, but Real Madrid managed to become the world's most popular football club through retaining its unique *Madrileño* identity. As the word *real* implies in Spanish, the club holds a royal charter, issued in the 1920s, from the king of Spain. More important, it is truly a local team and has been continuously owned by local shareholders, or *socios* (who, as of the 2009–2010 season, numbered 91,526 adult, junior, and senior members), since its inception. The club draws more than eighty thousand ticket holders to its iconic stadium for each of its forty games a year and is central to the culture and vitality of the city that gave it its name. Real Madrid's success is both local and global, virtual and physical—and rather than being in conflict, these realities reinforce each other.

With the rise of our increasingly global and interconnected world, marketers are encouraged to focus on the biggest picture possible—expanding brands throughout the world to achieve a leading global share. There is nothing inherently wrong in this approach, and the advances in technology have made this more practical than ever before. The danger lies when companies forget the importance of all other types of place. Global is glamorous and strategic, but when marketers focus solely on attaining it, they risk becoming irrelevant.

Former Speaker of the United States House of Representatives Thomas P. O'Neill Jr. once famously declared "All politics is local." The same is true for business. McDonald's spans the globe, but in the Philippines, Jollibee, a local fast-food chain, dominates the market. Google is a household word around the world and offers a search interface in more than 120 languages, but Yandex in Russia and Baidu in China are the local market share leaders. Local competitors and upstart entrepreneurs who have gained secure footholds in local markets, and who increasingly have access to cross-border capital and know-how, are sneaking up on global brands. That means businesses large and small must be local as well as global in order to succeed.

With this focus on the importance of local comes the opportunity to examine other ways in which marketers can use the concept of place strategically. In our view, place determines how consumers interact with a product or brand. From the arrangement of breakfast cereals on supermarket shelves to the ease of navigation and checkout in a digital store, place very powerfully and routinely influences our choice of brands—or whether to buy anything at all. On a larger scale, the competitive appeal of Charlotte versus Chicago, or Cancún versus Bali, determines where we choose to start a business or take a vacation. Customer relationships to places profoundly affect the business of marketing—they are fundamental to the ways in which every one of us organizes our lives.

Fundamentals of Place

Any marketer or business student from the last fifty years will be familiar with the 4Ps—product, price, promotion, and place—introduced by E. Jerome McCarthy in 1960 and widely adopted by other textbook authors.[3] In this formulation, "place" means the various physical distribution activities undertaken to make the product available to consumers. Nowadays, it is clear that this definition is much too narrow. Multiple aspects of place and location are relevant to marketing, and each of them must be considered for a brand to have the maximum impact in our connected world.

In our more inclusive view, the primary strands of place include the following:

Psychological Place

People have a web of mental associations with location. Consumers may attribute juiciness to oranges from Florida or associate a Dodge Durango with the rugged outdoors. Such associations carry over to product preferences in everything from where fruit comes from to which Web browser to click on.

Physical Place

Part of the marketer's job is to make products physically accessible to customers. Stores attract consumers through convenient location or proximity to other retailers. The structural characteristics and uses of space at retailers such as Nike and the Apple Store influence people's wants and motivate them to buy.

Virtual Place

Increasingly, consumers search for information or buy products online, in virtual places. Mobile devices with "geolocational" capabilities allow marketers to send tailored ads or electronic coupons to consumers keyed to where the consumer is located at a particular moment.

Geographic Place

In a significant contribution to local economies, consumers "buy" places—for example, in the form of a visit to France or to Spain—places that actively market themselves as travel destinations. Place and product become intertwined when destinations from Champagne to Madras lend their names to marketed goods.

Global Place

The best global brands, from IBM to McDonald's, are by design also the leading local brands, and vice versa; companies today must simultaneously market to multiple levels to create a virtual loop.

For marketers, managing all the elements of place includes physical distribution—that is, the activities that make products available in places where customers are. It includes retailing—selecting and designing places to present and sell goods to consumers, whether they are physical or virtual places. It includes consumer behavior and psychology—understanding and influencing how consumers make decisions based on a brand's associations with a place. It includes organizational strategy and structure—choosing where to market and setting managerial responsibilities for those places.

Tellingly, the 4Ps are often discussed as a sequence—first product, then price, and so on—rather than as overlapping and mutually dependent sets of activities. This encourages managers to focus on product development as the necessary strategic starting point for marketing planning. With place at the end of the line, merchandising and distribution issues are inevitably viewed and treated as more tactical in nature, considered only after the other three parts of the marketing program have been decided. Yet experience shows that treating place last can radically reduce the marketing opportunity. Treating place earlier prompted Procter & Gamble (P&G) to introduce 2x ultraconcentrated laundry detergent, which allowed twice as many bottles to be placed on the same shelf space. Place knowledge enabled Apple to reap enormous retail success with well-situated stores that can communicate the Apple experience to consumers by allowing them to touch and feel the products.

In this book, we will show how place is critical to nearly every marketing planning decision, and why place, now more than ever, cannot be an afterthought. We aim to concisely address all the aspects of place in marketing—from where a particular product should be placed on a supermarket shelf to how globally standardized versus locally adapted marketing programs should be balanced in a brand's overall strategy.

We Live in a Flat and Spiky, Globalized and Local World

In the past few years, we've been given mixed messages about how the world is arranged. Some scholars and pundits tell us the world is flat while others insist it's spiky. Some politicians and observers tell us that cultures and values are converging, while others point to cultural divergences that generate world conflict. Some praise globalization, while others point to its dangers. We're told consumers want to live in a digital cloud but still value the importance of physical touch.[4] Only one thing is certain: competing trends are pulling multinational firms in all directions at once.

This forces us to ask questions: Which of these ideas and trends will dominate, and where? Which matter most to marketers? Which should they be reacting to and planning for? The right answer is that there is no right answer. We must accept a world in which all of the above thinkers can be right, depending on the context, marketing purpose, and business model. Accepting this premise means accepting that place still matters, that the local is still as significant as the global, and vice versa. It means believing that IBM is successful because it creates "Solutions for a Small Planet," while HSBC attracts customers by being "The world's local bank."

Local marketing and global marketing must coexist. No global company is more quintessentially American than McDonald's or Coca-Cola—both of which may represent the first physical contact that some people have with things American. Yet even McDonald's cannot be a great global brand without being a great local brand. It could not penetrate, let alone dominate, markets the world over without expanding beyond its global core products and cultivating authentic local appeal. This has been a more gradual process in some markets than others—Europe accounts for 40 percent of revenues, while Asia Pacific, the Middle East, and Africa collectively account for less than a quarter. But almost every McDonald's outlet is locally owned and locally staffed, and, wherever possible, uses locally sourced supplies. Each franchisee is encouraged to invest in the local community; and the global hamburger leader goes to great lengths to customize menus to local tastes.[5]

Our Virtual and Physical World

Google is perhaps the ultimate "placeless" firm—all of its services and products are delivered to consumers worldwide via the "cloud." It apparently doesn't matter where Google offices or servers are as long as you can access its products whenever and wherever there's an online connection. Yet recently the firm paid a high price for thinking it was "beyond geography."[6] In January 2010, Google announced it was considering leaving China—both its cyberspace market and physical presence there—after discovering the Gmail accounts of Chinese political dissidents had been hacked. This was not the first time Google had a run-in with China; for years it had balked at having to comply with Chinese government censorship of search requests on its Chinese-language Web site. In the ensuing spat between Google and the Chinese government, few believe Google won. Meanwhile, the company faced invasion of privacy lawsuits in Germany after it photographed streetscapes featuring private homes for its Street View mapping product. Google, a company whose primary product has no physical form, had suddenly become firmly rooted in place.

The Internet and the mobile phone are the most recent in a long line of technological advances that have transformed marketing by lowering physical barriers of place. In the case of digitizable products (such as words or music), entire transactions—from production and distribution through purchase, delivery, and consumption—can occur in virtual space. And even for products that must be acquired in a physical form, online searching, ordering, and payment options fulfill many of the functions performed by traditional—that is, physical—retailers. The Internet has also transformed marketing communications and democratized the brand knowledge and expectations of consumers around the world by accelerating the spread of word-of-mouth and viral advertising, more so even than television.

But as the Google example shows, although cyberspace markets theoretically dispense with conventional geographical boundaries, in practice, geography still counts. Political boundaries with associated laws, regulations, taxes, and trade agreements still govern sellers and their digital or physical products. Relatively few online transactions cross national borders.

The geographical location features embedded in the latest communication technologies are further increasing the importance of place in the marketing mix. With great precision, these geolocation technologies are able to identify the location of a mobile phone and report it to the user, the phone company, or third parties. Firms can offer consumers ads and promotions based on their physical location. Sites like Yelp allow consumers in turn to submit geotagged reviews and photos (which verify that the reviewer actually visited the establishment in question) that increasingly make or break the success of restaurants, hotels, and other service businesses.

Integrate the Many Facets of Place

Real Madrid exists powerfully in psychological place, in physical place, and in virtual place. For the fans who are voting members of the club and who show up to cheer the team at every game, the Real Madrid brand occupies, next to family and friends, the most important place in their collective psyche, thanks to the emotional connections they share with the team. The place where they assemble, the Bernabéu Stadium, is an iconic location where countless championships have been won. It is open year-round, hosting concerts and other outside events. Visitors arrive from around the world to tour the stadium, to view the trophies in the club museum, and to buy merchandise at the store. To reach its ever-expanding fan base around the world, Real Madrid offers (in virtual space) a Web site, online news, and mobile apps for accessing game highlights and other services—some free, some paid.

As this example indicates, managing place has become more complicated than ever. In the early years of marketing as a formal discipline, most business remained local. Few companies achieved national distribution or a national brand. Later, as businesses grew, the focus was on reaching national scale—especially through improving the speed and efficiency of supply chains that link places. By the 1970s and 1980s, there were rising numbers of multinational corporations, and a commensurate expansion of the geographical footprints where marketers envisioned profitable business opportunities. The fall of the Berlin Wall in 1989 symbolized the opening up of new, formerly communist regimes to Western marketers. Businesses that had been multinational became global, with ever higher percentages of sales outside their domestic markets. The global stage of marketing brought an ongoing debate, ignited by Theodore Levitt, over the virtues of standardized global marketing programs versus the-then norm of local adaptation.[7] Levitt advocated global standardization on the grounds that consumers everywhere wanted the latest, most reliable, and highest quality products at the lowest prices. But experience taught nearly all global marketers that at least some elements of marketing programs required adaptation to local conditions; and these modifications could be adopted at sufficiently low cost to maintain profitability.

A decade or so later, large national and global marketers have started redefining their focus on place—away from global or universal place, and toward hyperlocal place. In this hyperlocal stage, much of the same technology that made possible the Internet and wireless telecommunications, when combined with the geolocation capabilities mentioned earlier, has enabled marketers to pinpoint consumers' geographic locations down to a city block or storefront. Falling costs of data collection, storage, and analysis, along with interactive telecommunications, have made it easier to target individual consumers or micro segments, for example, delivering micro bursts of electronic messages, including promotional discounts, to consumers as they browse individual store aisles. As well, geographic segmentation has gained in precision. With better information, quick manufacturing, and declining transportation costs, global marketers are able, under the same brand name, to tailor product assortments or customized versions of products to meet the demand preferences of different localities. Zara, the Spanish clothing company, monitors daily sales trends in each of its two thousand stores worldwide, sews up small batches of new fashions, and delivers replenishments customized to consumer demand trends in each of its stores.

Along with managing geographical expansion, marketers have needed to master the complexities of place from a psychological perspective. As businesses grew more sophisticated at understanding and shaping customer behavior, marketers at leading-edge consumer-goods firms, such as Procter & Gamble, increasingly wanted to know what goes on inside people's heads. Advertising evolved from extolling the functional benefits of products to forging emotional connections between consumers and brands, and establishing a position in psychological space. Actual or imagined places became interesting to consumer marketers in terms of the meanings people attached to brands associated with them—think of the many products whose ad imagery centered on slice-of-life messages from the suburban family home.

When the invention of the World Wide Web and sophisticated search engines helped spur widespread consumer adoption of the Internet in the 1990s, marketers needed to explore the frontier of virtual place. Many early Web sites were essentially online brochures. Increasingly, sites incorporated more sophisticated information and purchase transaction capabilities. Businesses pursued the prospect that everything would be available more cheaply and conveniently on the Internet, that more efficient, transnational supply chains would shave costs and time and supplant national and regional distributors, and that, thanks to cheap online marketing communications and easily spread word of mouth, consumers around the world would become aware of and would want the same global brands, and would engage with marketers in virtual online communities.

We believe the ease with which marketing organizations integrate all aspects of place and move seamlessly back and forth from the local geographical to the global, from the physical to the virtual, and from the functional to the psychological is a source of competitive advantage. Marketers need to have their products and services available in all the right locations; distribution—in both the virtual and physical worlds—is more critical than ever to marketing success. Marketers need to sense and respond to market, competitive, and customer dynamics—all of which vary in different geographies. Acquiring a more integrated knowledge of place enables businesses to better integrate place into marketing strategy and tactics.

Surveys of chief executives' priorities often reveal an undue emphasis in product innovation to drive growth. In fact, innovation in the other three dimensions of the marketing mix—price, promotion, and place—can also drive growth. The power of innovating around place to drive top-line growth was famously illustrated by the case of L'eggs panty hose. In the 1970s, panty hose could only be bought in department stores where customers had to search through disorganized displays of styles, colors, and sizes, often finding that their desired combination was out of stock. Enter L'eggs with no change in product quality, but a convenient change in place and a new system of distribution. The L'eggs brand was launched in supermarkets and drug stores, where free-standing displays were placed on consignment. This meant L'eggs salespeople were responsible for restocking them. The products were well organized and displayed in eye-catching color-coded packaging so consumers could quickly identify them. The physical form of the packaging lent its name to the brand and created a unique space in consumers' minds. To this day, L'eggs remains the number one brand of panty hose on the market.

Although place draws the least notice among the 4Ps, it deserves much more managerial attention. After all, place is where the buying transaction occurs. While Pepsi sells the same brands worldwide, it recognizes that winning the battle for worldwide market share happens at the local level one purchase at a time. Likewise, even in today's integrated world, almost all marketing is retail. For sure, some business-to-business transactions take the form of global procurement contracts and others involve sales of infrastructure projects and aircraft to national governments. But remember that 70 percent of the U.S. gross national product (GNP) is consumer driven. In some cases, consumer purchase decisions are in favor of global rather than local brands; increasingly, people are willing to buy online from remote suppliers. Nevertheless, the bulk of the economy remains local. Time and place utility remain important. And, following the financial crisis of 2008, we became perhaps more willing to trust the local neighborhood bank—with a physical branch on our local Main Street—than some national or global bank where we, as individual consumers, are of little consequence. When there's a problem, we need local service and support. That's why, for decades, State Farm Insurance with its nationwide network of agents, offices, and claims adjusters used this as its tagline: "Like a good neighbor, State Farm is there."

Place is a key consideration in allocating marketing communication expenditures. Local advertising historically has been, and remains, one of the best ways to reach consumers. Consider the automotive industry, consistently a heavy advertiser. In 2008 (the latest year for which full data were available at the time of writing this), local auto dealers accounted for about 40 percent of the approximately $14.7 billion combined total that automakers, dealer associations, and local dealers in the United States spent on advertising.[8] That same year, well over half of the expenditures by all advertisers on television, radio, newspapers, magazines, and the Internet was for local, nonnational media, including local broadcast and cable TV, local broadcast radio, local newspapers, and local online Web sites and listings.[9]

Managing multiple aspects of place well is at the heart of retailing. Retailers compete aggressively for the best locations, which depend on a host of factors—including traffic flow, the number of pedestrians and cars passing by at different times of day, the convenience of shopping, and the presence of complementary retail outlets. Dependable distribution from manufacturer to warehouse to store—along with reliable inventory management—is key to achieving cost efficiencies. Navigation within the store is important. Small changes in aisle placements or shelf displays can alter consumer purchase behaviors. The physical geography, seasonality, and other characteristics of where customers live determine, in part, what products they need. Increasingly, customers expect retailers to coordinate the experience of shopping at physical locations with the experience of shopping online.

To marketers trying to add value, relying on geographic (or demographic) segmentation can seem rather obvious and far less interesting than segmenting consumers according to lifestyles, attitudes and interests, or media usage. But place remains one of the most reliable bases for targeting and positioning decisions. There are still social and cultural differences from one geographic region to another.[10] Geographic segmentation serves as a useful surrogate for consumer lifestyles and provides addressability of marketing communications to where people live or shop.

One significant challenge for managers is that much of what is known about place was learned in the past, in the United States and other industrialized countries. That knowledge has to be constantly updated and expanded to adapt to new geographies and different levels of development. For example, how much of what we know about supply chains and distribution channels applies in various types of developing countries? What are the best strategies for retail location and geographic expansion? Take the situation of Briggs & Stratton, the U.S.

maker of lawn mowers, which is seeking growth in overseas markets as demand stagnates in suburban America: Briggs & Stratton identified a market in rural China for rice harvesters and planters that incorporate its engines. Now, though, the challenge is finding a set of rural distributors able to develop the market and, among other tasks, obtain government endorsements permitting farmers to receive substantial subsidies on purchases.[11]

For managers of any size business, the greatest challenge is being able to seamlessly mesh all the various dimensions of place. In our ideal world, for any particular geographical market, ranging from the micro to global scale, a brand manager would be able to overlay information on the physical presence of the brand, its virtual presence, and its psychological meanings—and make better decisions as a result.

Be Intelligently Local

Real Madrid is vital to a vibrant Madrid, and vice versa. Millions of tourists visit Madrid each year just to see Real Madrid play, while a strong base of season ticket holders and dues-paying members is linked to the health of the local economy. For years, the club has sponsored extensive outreach programs to the community, particularly among young people and in the prison population. The Real Madrid Foundation now sponsors programs that combine sports, education, health, and the promotion of peaceful values for children and teenagers in Central and South America, the Middle East, Africa, and, most recently, China.

A critical competitive advantage for marketers will be a renewed focus on place at the local level. This new focus on local treats market areas not as a collection of atomistic individual consumers nor as administratively convenient subdivisions of countries or regions, but as places defined by social interrelationships, sets of common tastes and values, and also particular geographical, cultural, and political characteristics.

When Hillary Clinton's *It Takes a Village* was published in 1996, some dismissed the premise as anachronistic in an age of increasing globalization and individualism. Clinton, who took the title from an African proverb, noted:

The sage who first offered that proverb would undoubtedly be bewildered by what constitutes the modern village. In earlier times and places—and until recently in our own culture—the "village" meant an actual geographic place where individuals and families lived and worked together. To many people the word still conjures up a road sign that reads, "Hometown U.S.A., pop. 5,340," followed by emblems of the local churches and civic clubs. For most of us, though, the village doesn't look like that anymore. In fact, it's difficult to paint a picture of the modern village, so frantic and fragmented has much of our culture become. Extended families rarely live in the same town, let alone the same house. In many communities, crime and fear keep us behind locked doors. Where we used to chat with neighbors on stoops and porches, now we watch videos in our darkened living rooms. Instead of strolling down Main Street, we spend hours in automobiles and at anonymous shopping malls.[12]

In the years since the book's publication, Facebook, Myspace, LinkedIn, and other social networking sites have added geographically agnostic virtual communities to the list of forces weakening the importance of social ties based on face-to-face proximity. The huge popularity of these sites reflects people's drive to gossip and to share—or "overshare"— parts of their lives with online "friends"; everyone has rushed to predict how social networking sites will forever change our interactions with one another. Yet now that the novelty has worn off, we predict these sites will increasingly be viewed as incomplete substitutes for the physical presence of friends and neighbors, or for the network of social, cultural, and political institutions of an actual village, town, or city. To use a blunt example, an e-community is no substitute when you break your leg and need help—at least not unless that e-community is tightly linked to physical community.

Although modern mass marketing is sometimes blamed for the dissolution of social bonds in the traditional village or urban neighborhood community, marketing, as we argued in a previous book, *Greater Good: How Good Marketing Makes for Better Democracy*, may also be used to nourish local community.[13] Howard Schultz conceived Starbucks as the third social place (after home and family; work place and col-leagues) where members of a community could relax or spend time with friends. In the United States, bars provided such a place for males, but were not as gender neutral as British pubs, or "locals." Schultz also wanted Starbucks to assume the role of the "neighborhood porch." Selling good quality coffee was just one element of selling a premium social experience; it was really about place. And although headquarters set design and quality standards, not every store was the same. Store format, design and menu selection (especially food items) were adapted to local market needs. Schultz made the point that Starbucks doesn't reach customers through five thousand stores, it reaches customers through one store five thousand times.

The most successful global marketers will be, like Schultz, intelligently local. As corporations become more national, multinational, or global, they serve more customers in more locations. Not all these customers have the same needs, desires, or preferences, especially when coming from diverse cultural backgrounds. Local knowledge thus confers a signifi-cant advantage in satisfying consumers. Moreover, given a choice between two global brands that are comparable in price and quality, consumers are more likely to choose the company they perceive to be more socially responsible in the local community.[14] By respecting local values and local tastes, by rooting themselves in the community, global brands broaden their appeal and build deeper trust with their con-sumers.

The "new localism," as described by Joel Kotkin,[15] is why global brands like Pepsi are spending so much time these days on connecting with local communities. Pepsi's Refresh Project, the centerpiece of its 2010 marketing effort, was all about celebrating and funding local projects. Consumers enlisted their social networks to vote for pet projects that competed for Pepsi grants. Local Pepsi bottlers were motivated by the campaign and their sales forces achieved better and more frequent placement of in-store promotional displays. Grant-seeking campaigns gained publicity in local media. By November 2010, forty-six million votes had been cast, over three hundred projects had been funded, and Pepsi planned to extend Refresh beyond the United States to other markets in 2011.

We live in an increasingly interconnected global economy. But that does not mean we all want to be global citizens. Indeed, many of us cherish our local roots, our neighborhoods and communities because that is where we spend the bulk of our time. The economic recession has accentuated our need to stay close to home, rekindling family ties and local friendships. Fewer Americans moved in 2008 than in 1962. Part of this can be explained by the slump in the housing market, but it's also true that economic uncertainty dissuades people from making big changes. When times are good, we feel that we can conquer the world. When times are tough, we seek assurance in familiar faces and familiar places. To understand today's consumers, we must understand their connections to place.

We do not contend that multinationals should abandon

global marketing principles. The equity of global brands is enormous, and economies of scale are not to be dismissed. But there are comparatively few cases where a global brand pushing a standardized global product is the optimal marketing strategy. More often, the norm will be a global brand with standardized positioning but localized product formulas: witness Colgate-Palmolive's adaptation of toothpastes to local flavor and consistency preferences—such as salt and tea flavors in China and powder instead of paste in India. Colgate's marketing adaptations are effective because the ratio of adaptation costs to product sales is quite low; moreover, strong global brands like Colgate often have deep pockets that allow them to invest in tailoring products to local tastes. Indeed, among global companies, Colgate stands out in its level of attention to local adaptation. It understands the trade-off between speed to market, adaptation costs, and the upside sales and profit benefits of getting it right for the local consumer. Procter & Gamble world headquarters manages its Crest brand with a tighter rein than Colgate, but P&G, while a close competitor of Colgate in the United States, trails substantially in the global market share for oral care—capturing about 20 percent share versus Colgate's 44 percent.

Being intelligently local includes a greater role for local management. Coca-Cola may have exaggerated when CEO Douglas Daft announced in March 2000 that the company's new marketing strategy would be "think local, act local." But the Australian-born Daft clearly saw a need for less centralized decision making and greater local autonomy that would help Coca-Cola to attract, motivate, and retain the best local business talent. Toyota offers a recent example of a global company that suffered enormous sales losses and reputational damage in the United States by reacting too slowly to evidence of quality defects, which happened, in part, because Tokyo headquarters overly limited the authority of executives in the United States.[16]

A Road Map for This Book

In this book, we'll explore how and why place matters to marketers, and how companies can navigate the contradictions of a world where location can matter both more and less than ever. We start with an exploration of psychological and mental place—the places where brand meanings reside and marketing communications are processed. Consumers have strong mental associations with places and place images that carry over to product preferences; these associations can be leveraged, or skirted, to the marketer's advantage.

Next we proceed to the physical environment and look at the ways in which the physical characteristics of places influence people's wants and needs and how the smart design of physical places—with an emphasis on retail stores—attracts and motivates consumers to buy.

Chapter Three builds on these perspectives as they apply to virtual space. We examine both the parallels and the differences between online marketplaces and virtual marketplaces.

In particular, we show how the spread of mobile devices with geolocational capabilities and deep information on customer preferences lead to delivery of specialized products keyed to where the consumer is located.

Chapter Four takes a different turn. Here we view places as things that can be marketed. Increasingly, places like nations, states, and towns market themselves to attract visitors and investors. Countries also market themselves in the form of "public diplomacy" programs to achieve foreign policy goals.

Finally, we offer our perspectives on global place. We focus on the strategies used by companies that are simultaneously marketing at the national and global levels. We also explore the challenges faced by marketing managements as they try to bridge local and global scales of operation.

All these strands of place are tightly woven together in businesses poised to grow in the global economy. To be sure, places gain their particular flavor not only because of their geography but because of who lives (and buys) there. As the leading fashion designer Sir David Tang sensibly put it: "It's not the place but the people that count."[17] Yet the founder of the Shanghai Tang brand of apparel and accessories clearly understood the way in which a place name can function as a marketing tool. By capitalizing on the fashion reputation of Asia's leading international city, Tang signals that his designs are exotic, chic, and exciting. In today's globally interconnected world there are countless Shanghai Tangs, exploiting local reputation to garner global appeal.

Chapter 1

MANAGING PSYCHOLOGICAL PLACE

Our sense of self develops in part through our relationships to the places where we grew up, where we have lived, and where special events have occurred. Our attachments to place are inseparable from social relationships. Our place of origin—revealed in our words, our dress, and our behaviors—enables us to identify with other members of the same tribe. That can be a source of comfort, and it can be nourished by savvy marketers in a globally mobile society.

In addition to the places known personally, people also develop associations with places they've only heard about, which may carry positive or negative connotations, and which may shade consumers' evaluations and willingness to purchase. France is associated with art, music, food, and wine; and plenty of marketers—from fashion houses to cheese makers—leverage these associations to their benefit. In contrast, products from Colombia or banks from Nigeria have to fight an uphill reputational battle because people associate these places with crime, poverty, and corruption. Companies need to think of creative ways to avoid such negative associations. For example, when El Salvador was embroiled in a civil war in the 1980s and 1990s, Hilasal, a leading global manufacturer of luxury beach towels headquartered there, set up an import company in Miami, under the logic that U.S. department store buyers would not feel confident in the company's ability to meet delivery deadlines from a war zone.

But the psychology of place extends well beyond geographic relationships. Place can also be a metaphor for status, whether social or professional. By definition, the place we want to be is aspirational; it influences our decisions on what neighborhood to live in, what lifestyle to adopt, and what products and services to buy. Places used as the settings in commercials— for products ranging from soup to travel—typically appear a cut above the average home or trip destination. Such images tap less into where we are than where we want to be.

This chapter explores the psychology of place as it relates to consumer identity, needs, and preferences, and how people organize and classify brands in mental space. Understanding these psychological factors can offer commercial brands a leg up as they fight along with the many other claimants, such as family, friends, workplace, religious, and political affiliations for attention and loyalty. The brands that rise to the top must then wage a secondary battle for the most favorable locations in our mental representations of relative brand positions and interconnections.

As we will see, sophisticated algorithms in the hands of market researchers can generate positioning maps that show how people individually and collectively position one brand in relation to another. Such positioning maps are indispensable in analyzing sets of products or market segments and enabling managers to clearly visualize strategic opportunities. They are also valuable for refining marketing programs for existing products or defining the programs for new products.

Place Is Part of Self

"Where do you live?" or "Where are you from?" are often among the initial questions we ask when we meet someone for the first time. We do this in a natural, polite search for common ground. Perhaps we may have visited that place or know someone from there or have seen something about it on the news. We ask in order to help ourselves piece together the identity of the person we're talking to. The answer may signify friend or foe, stranger or compatriot, one of us or one of them. In any case, we assume that someone's place of origin tells us something relevant about the person himself or at least gives us a point of reference from which to extend the conversation.

How we answer the question "Where are you from?" often depends on the context and who is asking. At an academic conference, you might answer "Harvard." Meeting a stranger in a foreign land, you might say the "United States" or, if you thought they knew the States in more detail, you might say "Boston" even if you live in a suburb. The closer the proximity to where the question is asked, the more specific the answer. If in Massachusetts, you're likely to respond by saying "Cambridge" rather than "Boston." And, if asked on the streets of Cambridge, you're likely to mention the specific neighborhood or street.

There is also the more pointed, "Where's home?" This can be a difficult question for someone who has lived in many places or changed his or her citizenship, but in most cases we fall back on the place where we were born or spent most of our childhood, even though current relationships—personal and professional—may be centered elsewhere. For some in the global economy—such as those born in one country, educated in a second, working in a third, or with parents of different nationalities and families spread across countries and continents—national boundaries may be less relevant. But no matter the degree of globalization and the cross-border and cross-cultural integration that has ensued, our home still defines us.

In other words, personal identity incorporates a geography with many layers. The relative importance of street, neighborhood, city, region, country, and continent in our articulation of geographic identity varies depending on our own life passage. It depends on where we think we have come from, not just in fact but in terms of the relative influence of the places we have been. It depends on the context in which the question is asked, the nature and purpose of the questioner, our own desires as to how we wish to be perceived, and our attachment to place. All these layers of identity are possible points of connection for marketers. Deep inside a hockey mom in Minnesota there may still be a sixteen-year-old "California Girl."

Place attachment occurs at the scale of dwelling place, community, region, and country; and it plays a role in individual, group, or cultural self-identity and self-esteem.[1] Nationality or town of origin serves as a badge to affiliate us with a certain group and differentiate us from others in the global melting pot. With this badge come loyalties and obligations: beliefs you are expected to hold and rivalries you are expected to honor. It is a potent factor in world politics: witness the Balkans, Israel, and Palestine. Strong social attachment to place also serves as a cultural glue that motivates groups to endure and rebuild through major environmental disasters rather than move on.[2] The importance of such badges has been understood by sports marketers at least since the inauguration of the Olympic Games. If you're from Boston, you're presumed to be an ardent member of the Red Sox Nation and a proud foe of the New York Yankees.

Regional affiliation and badgelike effects also matter for product brands. Recent research by Bart Bronnenberg and colleagues, reported in a University of Chicago paper, found that places where consumers have lived in the past have a significant impact on current brand preferences. In fact, the preferences for brands that were popular in places where the consumer lived previously "are highly persistent once formed, with experiences 50 years in the past still exerting a significant effect on current consumption." As evidence of the badge effect, the persistence of brand preference was higher for those products where consumption is highly visible to other people.[3] For example, products such as beverages and chips tend to be more socially visible than toothpaste or cold remedies.

All this is not to say that increasing cosmopolitanism hasn't altered place affiliations. In the twenty-first century, many of us increasingly see the whole planet as our place. A 2009 survey by the University of Maryland asked people in twenty-one countries whether they considered themselves more a citizen of their country, more a citizen of the world, or both equally. Surprisingly, half of the French respondents and substantial numbers elsewhere see themselves as either a citizen of the world or both equally. Not surprisingly, those who are younger, more educated, know people from other countries, or have traveled outside of their country are more likely to see themselves as global citizens.[4] Most young people today (other than those in Africa, the Middle East, and remnants of the Iron Curtain) have not known cross-border conflict; so, perhaps, because they have not had to rely on a nation or tribe to ensure their safety, they are more inclined to define themselves in supranational terms. Another factor may be the rise of the green movement and the ethos that everyone on the planet is responsible for its fate. More and more people around the world (if not in the United States) are listening to the message that global climate change and other environmental problems cannot be solved on a piecemeal basis but require the nations and corporations of the world to work together—anywhere it's necessary.

Place Is Intrinsic to the Human Experience

Place runs deep in the human experience. At a fundamental biological level, human senses are focused on establishing our location and the locations of other people and objects. Sight, hearing, touch, and smell all orient the organism to the surrounding environment. Learning the relation of self to place is a crucial step in the development of our brains as infants. Swiss psychologist Jean Piaget showed how a child's visual and spatial thinking progresses in stages from self-centric to other-centric space and gains increasing comprehension of points, routes, and object relationships.[5] Conversely, spatial disorientation, not recognizing places, and a tendency to wander and get lost is one mark of the deterioration of self-identity due to Alzheimer's or Parkinson's diseases.

From an evolutionary perspective, territorial individuals and groups—humans and other animals—mark or personalize a space and defend it from encroachment in order to secure resources essential for survival. Exploring, naming, classifying, and reasoning about geographical features of the environment are inherent human tendencies.[6] We have a strong desire to know where we are, to orient ourselves, to determine where lies safety and where lies danger.[7] The disciplines of urban design and architecture take these needs as basic principles. City planners are concerned with the "legibility" of places—that is, people's ability to comprehend public places and to form mental maps that help steer them through these spaces. The Hollywood trope of an unseen menace lurking in a parking garage derives its power to scare from the hostility of a place that does not fulfill these needs.

Many cultures view certain places as sacred and as an essential part of their identity.[8] Both Chinese Buddhism and the Navajo religion of the American Southwest contain beliefs in four sacred mountains. For the Navajos, these peaks to the north, east, south, and west define their traditional homeland. In the secular realm, we may express a similar sense of special place by means of symbols or abstractions—such as an idealized New England town with steeples and white clapboard houses or a nineteenth-century painting of sublime nature replete with lofty Alps and plunging cascades.[9] In print ads and television commercials, such symbolic images of place serve as a convenient shorthand for linking a product to a set of consumer values.

We may feel part of a place—comfortably at home there— or we may feel like an outsider. These feelings grow out of direct experience with both the physical (objects, spaces, and places) and social (people and relationships) aspects of the environment, which in turn are merged with a lifetime's worth of images, ideas, and memories. Among these, for instance, are our culturally-influenced norms about crowding and personal expression. Depending on the context—intimate, personal, social, or public—we are comfortable with varying zones of personal space. We may value one space in the home as an opportunity for privacy and another—say, the kitchen—

as an opportunity to demonstrate mastery of a skill or to be with family. Different places provide opportunities to present different aspects of self-identity or perhaps to acquire new ones.[10] Astute retailers of products such as home furnishings, apparel, accessories, and sporting goods design compelling store environments intended to foster such explorations of identity.

Most of us also adapt our behaviors to the place we are at any given moment. We learn that behaviors that are appropriate in one place may not be elsewhere. Moreover, we create places that constitute "behavior settings" that can provide social order and continuity. Churches, schools, and grocery stores, for example, are designed to promote particular patterns of behavior among persons and objects in that setting, which continue over time even though individual participants come and go.[11]

The Role of Place in Acquisitions

Clearly, physical geography and physical space influence our perceptions of what products we need. Try selling snow blowers to consumers in Phoenix or bulk packages of paper towels to apartment dwellers in Tokyo. Second, the people in the places where we spend our daily lives—family, colleagues, neighbors—also shape our wants and preferences. Third, our mental associations with place—with the here and the there— mold our needs, wants, desires, and decisions. For example, the country of origin for a product or brand can connote mediocrity or excellence. California wine may be popular in the United States, but try selling it to a Parisian. Taken together, these aspects of place powerfully influence consumers' brand attitudes and preferences.

For nearly any business, geographical location combined with economic, sociological, attitudinal, or behavioral data is one of the most useful forms of market segmentation, in part because marketers using it know where to look for consumers in the desirable segments. Joel Garreau's *Nine Nations of North America* popularized the idea that the United States and bordering areas of Mexico and Canada comprise regions with distinctive economies, cultures, and prisms through which inhabitants view the world.[12] These regions transcend the traditional regional, state, and national boundaries conventionally used by marketers and social commentators. While Garreau has had to revise his predictions, his original thesis remains a valuable corrective to more simplistic divisions of the nation into areas such as the Northeast, South, and Midwest, and it is a good starting point for further segmentation. The approach has spawned many other mappings, including the "nine nations of China."[13]

At a much more granular level, the PRIZM segmentation system from the Claritas market research firm melds demographic, consumer behavior, and geographic data to group U.S. households into sixty-six distinct segments, including "God's Country," "Pools and Patios," and "Home Sweet Home."[14] Each segment is characterized by lifestyle, media usage, product likes and dislikes, and purchase behavior.

Each consumer segment may comprise subsegments located in different parts of the country, and can be mapped onto geographic areas down to zip code or census-block levels. For example, the "Young Digerati" segment includes "the nation's tech-savvy singles and couples living in fashionable neighborhoods on the urban fringe. Affluent, highly educated and ethnically mixed, 'Young Digerati' communities are typically filled with trendy apartments and condos, fitness clubs, clothing boutiques, casual restaurants and all types of bars—from juice to coffee to microbrew."[15]

Attachment to home—as evidenced by names of the "Pools and Patios" and "Home Sweet Home" PRIZM segments—is one of the most potent motivators of the way we behave as consumers. The idealized dwelling place provides shelter, safety, and privacy; it nurtures the family; conveys qualities of individual taste and status to others; and is an outlet for creativity and self-expression. From such mundane items as cleaning sprays to a new sofa to the purchase of a house, home-related purchases invoke these sorts of powerful conscious or unconscious associations. We respond to the advertising promises that our home will be as impeccably clean and healthy as the images shown in the ad. When the outside world seems difficult or harsh, the common instinct is to retreat to the nest and center our activities and purchases on that environment.

Yet if many consumers long for the familiarity of "here," as represented by the home, they also are susceptible to the "grass is greener" phenomenon. Within the highly mobile society of the United States, the promise of a better place to live is a powerful motivator of consumer behavior. At age eighteen, an American can expect to move, on average, eighteen times in his or her lifetime. About 12.5 percent of the population moved to a new residence in 2009. Some moved for job-related or family concerns; but seventeen million people, or 46 percent of movers, said they moved because they wanted to own a home or live in a better neighborhood.[16] Seeking a comfortable lifestyle, migratory "snowbird" retirees spend the winter months in the Sunbelt and the remainder of the year in the north.

Another powerful motivator is a longing for the excitement and allure of the "there." Here may be familiar and safe, but the foreign and exotic has its own appeal. An interest in experimentation and the multiethnic diversity of many major cities have greatly expanded consumer appreciation of foreign cuisines, consumed not only in authentically ethnic or upscale specialty restaurants but translated to the Taco Bell, Pizza Hut, and Panda Express fast-food restaurant chains as well. Of course, in Beijing, it is McDonald's that may seem exotic and novel. Even in these quick-serve environments, the customer is often buying into the ambience and the perceived personality of the country associated with the menu. Store fixtures and point-of-sale displays are designed to complement the nationality of the cuisine.

Other people respond to a desire to traverse barriers between the here and the there so that "the world's mine oyster." We love automobiles both because they transport us from point A to point B and because they are a mobile place of refuge, cocooning us wherever we go. International travel is popular because it permits first-hand exposure to different cultures. Tourists can choose among travel packages or itineraries that offer different levels of comfort or adventure. Young people, on average, are willing to travel more readily and to experiment with new experiences. For the more sedentary, an abiding interest in other places is satisfied by books and magazines, film, or even simulacrums such as Disney's Epcot Center.

Attitudes toward the planet, or self-identification as a global citizen or as a steward of a place, seem increasingly to affect everyday consumption decisions. Countering the rise of global sourcing and cross-border trade, the green movement is contributing to a surge of interest among consumers from wealthier countries in locally sourced and organically produced fresh produce. In the United States, upmarket supermarket chains like Whole Foods and Wild Oats capitalize on this trend. So does Waitrose in Great Britain. Farmers' markets are a common Saturday morning sight in many towns around the country. There is a growing segment of consumers willing to pay a price premium for fresh, locally grown, and potentially tastier food than "corporate" food grown with the aid of fertilizers and shipped for several days from one coast to another. Health is not the only value. Buyers derive satisfaction from supporting farmers in their local communities, and the buying process at farm stands and farmers' markets is often more socially engaging than shopping in a supermarket.

Place and Brands

Because attachment to place is so profound a part of human experience, consumers often form a strong, favorable emotional response to brands that incorporate place imagery in their names or advertising. Brands like Cascade, Tide, Dawn, Febreze, Irish Spring, Mountain Dew, Klondike, Surf, Alpine, Pontiac, Dodge Durango, Chrysler Aspen, Subaru Outback, Chevrolet Tahoe, and Toyota Tacoma associate themselves with natural features of the environment or special places. The classic advertising for Marlboro cigarettes relied on the appeal, not just of the rugged Marlboro man, but also the archetypal west of the open range. Brands such as the Shangri-La hotel chain leverage the names of fictional, mythical places that powerfully evoke idealized qualities. Hermes nearly always mentions Paris. The Shanghai Tang fashion brand sells the most upscale Chinese apparel. Jack Daniel's identifies itself as Tennessee whiskey.

But brands do not have to be upscale or idealized to connect with a consumer or convey authenticity. Newcastle Brown Ale, for example, was brewed in and took its name from Newcastle upon Tyne in the northeast of England. Links to the industrial, urban, working-class values and traditions of its place of origin are an important component of the brand imagery and brand meaning of the full-flavored bottled ale. A silhouette of the city skyline appears on the label. Advertising campaigns have featured the local nickname for the brew—"a bottle of dog"—and local consumption practices: pouring it from the cold bottle into a half-pint glass to maintain a head and keep it cool. In the 1990s, the ale received a Protected Geographical Indication from the European Union, which was later revoked when the brewery moved from Newcastle. By then, however, Newcastle Brown Ale led the UK market for bottled ale sold in pubs.[17]

In an era of outsourcing and globalized production, there remain product categories where it pays marketers to ensure that superior expertise is still widely associated with a particular place. Champagne is a prominent example. French manufacturers and regulators fiercely limit the right to use the champagne nomenclature to sparkling wines produced in the Champagne region of France. Competing products include high-quality sparkling wines from Spain and California, but none have been able to challenge the cachet (and price premium) of champagne. The French have achieved control by restricting the "champagne" designation to a unique geographic area rather than by designating the process of production, which can be imitated. As is also the case with Bordeaux and Burgundy wines, the geographic area of Champagne has become an umbrella brand in its own right, under which various individual producers happily compete. The geographic restriction has the further advantage of setting a limit on supply. This short supply contributes to the price premium often achieved by French champagne and wines over blind-taste-test comparables from other countries. Newer wine-producing areas have followed in French footsteps.

Makers of Australian Shiraz and Argentinian Malbec wines have developed these into umbrella brands that convey a certain style and consistency of quality.

Other beverage categories have witnessed similar, though less sustained, examples of increases in demand and/or price based on place of manufacture. In the 1980s, Coors beer became highly popular on college campuses. Brewed only in one place—Golden, Colorado—Coors reputedly derived a special taste from the purity of the water in the Colorado Rockies. These positive consumer perceptions about Colorado, along with limited distribution to east of the Mississippi from the single plant, enabled Coors beer to command a price premium. Kona coffee, produced in limited quantities on specially designated mountain slopes on Hawaii's Big Island, remains one of the most expensive and exclusive coffees in the world.

Champagne, Coors, and Newcastle Brown Ale have one thing in common. Not only do they use geography as an identifier, but they consistently leverage it in their marketing to differentiate themselves and create perceptions of superiority. Since food is among the most culture-bound of categories and food preparation is often a function of locally available ingredients and ancient recipes, it is here that we frequently find beneficial uses of geographic-origin-based branding. A few examples are Cornish pasties, Wellfleet oysters, Chicago deep dish pizza, and Gruyère cheese. Scotland, Norway, and Alaska are seen as the best sources of salmon, though most consumers now know that whether or not the salmon is caught wild or farm raised is more important to its quality.

Typically, the product categories where place of origin counts most are those where consumers have, over many decades, developed the perception that the special skills needed to achieve excellence are clustered in a particular place. Such a perception is reinforced when leading global brands in the category are headquartered there. Hence, BMW and Mercedes-Benz give Germany its reputation for automobile engineering, while Armani and Brioni give Italy its reputation for men's suits. Many luxury brands, such as Cartier and Prada, are owned privately by distinguished European families to whom maintaining excellence in craftsmanship is more important than sales growth; these brands are treasured as part of the national patrimony.

As corporations grow increasingly supranational, it is not uncommon for a brand strongly associated with one country to be acquired by foreign owners. When the Swedish-headquartered Volvo Car Corporation was bought, first by U.S. automaker Ford Motor, and then a decade later by Hong Kong–based Zhejiang Geely Holding, the new owners retained headquarters and some manufacturing in Sweden. However, as the linkage to Sweden fades, the company may quite well see a weakening of consumers' associations with Volvo + Sweden = safe and strongly built. Similarly, the acquisition of the iconic British car makers Land Rover and Jaguar by Tata Motors of India may erode their luxury positioning, because India is not known for automotive excellence.

Note though, in many, if not most, product categories, even when the brand carries place-based identifiers, the actual place of manufacture is less important than other markers.[18] The UK-based Foster company that made Reebok shoes became the American company Reebok International when the Reebok brand's U.S. distributor bought it out in 1981. The company controlled the design, marketing, and branding functions, but an increasing percentage of the shoes were made by subcontractors in Korea. What did not change was that all Reebok shoes and shoe boxes continued to carry the Union Jack logo. Young consumers, far from being confused or concerned that the shoes of an American company carried the British flag and were made in Korea, could not buy enough of them.

In fact, the flood of outsourcing has made it nearly impossible for consumers or business buyers—and international trade regulators—to identify country of origin with any degree of precision. Many BMW cars—usually the more junior and less technically complex products in the range—are no longer built in Germany. McKinsey is an American consulting firm, but over half of its professional consultants are non-American. Only 10 percent by value of the parts in Boeing's new Dreamliner aircraft is sourced in the United States.

In all these cases, the power of brand trust is expected to override any doubts customers might have as a result of products being sourced from multiple countries. Consumers are more concerned about the country or place of design and quality oversight than the country or place of manufacture. Apple's iPods, iPhones, and iPads deemphasize place of manufacture and instead carry the label "Designed by Apple in

California." An international airline might not readily purchase an entire airliner made in China but will trust the American company Boeing to selectively source some components from Chinese factories, ensure their quality, and integrate them properly in the assembly process. Likewise, few consumers will object to flying the Boeing 787 Dreamliner on the grounds that the parts are sourced from more than twenty countries and only 10 percent of the plane's components are American made. What is important is Boeing's long-standing track record of airplane design—and for some consumers, the comparative unfamiliarity with the European Airbus.

Positioning Brands in Mental Space

To clarify how consumers relate to products and brands, it is instructive to map the places these occupy in mental space. Like maps of physical terrain, maps of mental space contain nodes and pathways, neighborhoods and distances. For example, one consumer's mental map tightly clusters together the Dell, Hewlett-Packard, Toshiba, and Acer personal computer brands. Hewlett-Packard is linked to the construct of "printers," and Dell to the construct of "customization." In this same map, the Apple brand stands by itself and is "closer" in that it comes to mind first. It also has strong links to the iPod music player and the iPhone smartphone. Sony and Lenovo form a more distant cluster with sparse, weak links to the rest of the personal computer space.

LIBRARY, UNIVERSITY OF CHESTER

Mental maps are formed or revised when a consumer is exposed to advertising or other information about a brand, and that information becomes incorporated into memory. They are activated when a consumer seeks to fulfill needs and wants through making a brand choice, and, in the process, retrieves stored information. In the detergent aisle, for example, making a choice is easier and faster when the mind travels along a well-established path to a handful of brands and product variants that fit well with the type of washing machine owned and the available storage space.

Everything marketers have learned about brand equity in the past twenty years reinforces the importance of positioning the brand in mental space. Brands should be prominent and close, distinctive but associated with a particular product class or consumer need, and strongly linked to favorable thoughts and associations.[19] The most effective links are two-way: thinking about buying car insurance evokes GEICO, and the mention of GEICO activates impressions of affordable car insurance with great service. Google is synonymous with finding information on the Web and Xerox is still used as the verb for making photocopies long after competitors like Canon took a big chunk of the market. Black & Decker lost this strong two-way link after overextending from the toolshed and garage to the kitchen.

Some of the stimuli that form mental maps about brands are bound to be highly personal and idiosyncratic. But others are the result of careful brand management. Al Ries and Jack Trout's classic from 1986, *Positioning: The Battle for Your Mind*, stressed the importance of establishing a unique position in the minds of consumers in a marketplace crowded with brands and advertisements all competing for attention.[20] According to Ries and Trout, most mind share goes to just one or two leader brands in a category—often because they were there first. Coca-Cola, for instance, has consistently led Pepsi and far outdistanced other colas. To have any hope of displacing the leader, Ries and Trout advised follower brands to concentrate on finding an empty niche in the market that they could be the first to occupy. They also suggested choosing a brand name that is distinct, memorable, and descriptive of the product. This is quite consistent with associating a brand name with a particular place—such as a place of origin (for example, Yoplait sounds French); a place where its benefits are obviously relevant (for example, Arizona iced teas introduced by a company based in New York); or primary place of business or market scope (for example, Bank of America).

Environmental cues also play a significant role in the activation of mental maps. Psychologists are concluding that, in everyday life, people encounter triggers that can activate or "prime" brain circuits that subconsciously influence evaluations or choices. For instance, subjects in an experiment run by Yale psychologists were handed a cup of either warm or iced coffee to hold momentarily. Afterwards, those holding the warm cup were more apt to view a hypothetical person described to them as having a warm personality; those holding the cold cup were more apt to think the same description indicated a cold personality.[21] In another experiment, people consuming a biscuit were more apt to clear the crumbs away when the room held a faint odor of cleaning fluid. Such findings underscore the significant role of packaging, merchandising, and other cues in the store environment on consumers' purchase decisions.

Brand Positioning Tools

Perceptual maps are widely used by marketers who want to understand how consumers perceive the relative similarities and differences among brands, and to discern the attributes that are most important to consumers in discriminating among them. Such maps also help identify "white spaces"— opportunities to introduce new products into a category in order to serve unmet needs.

Market researchers can turn to a variety of methods and plotting techniques to capture consumers' mental maps. One approach is to measure consumers' perceptions of the brands within a product category along two or three pre-specified dimensions and then to display the data on a graph. The results show which perceptual spaces brands occupy and which brands are close to or distant from each other. Some forms of multidimensional scaling simply ask consumers how similar brands or products are to each other and/or what their preferences are for each. Researchers can then mathematically infer the implicit dimensions and ratings consumers use to position the brands— the relative importance of dimensions can be indicated by the relative strength of vectors (see Figure 1). Perhaps the simplest

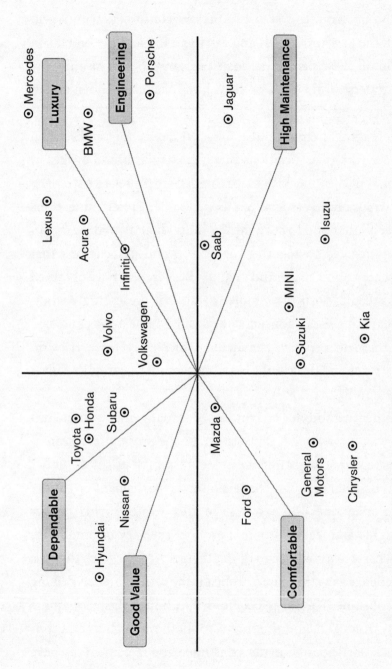

FIGURE 1. Perceptual Map of Brand Image (Hypothetical) with Attribute Vectors

way to go about this is just to present consumers with a grid (with the axes unlabeled) and ask them to place the brands on it. On all these perceptual maps, researchers can also display consumers' ideal points, or the volume of consumer demand in various parts of the space.

Perceptual maps are also a useful device for representing the network of associations that a particular brand evokes in a consumer's mind. Such maps can display the relative strength of various brand associations as well as their interconnections to each other and to core values. Individual mental maps can be aggregated to identify the core brand associations that most contribute to a brand's equity. Researchers have obtained good results with the simple method of presenting participants with a list of concepts or possible associations and asking them to produce a map on which they place relevant constructs and draw links between them.[22] (A sample result is shown in Figure 2.)

Other methods for arriving at these maps employ visual imagery as well as verbal expressions. In one procedure, researchers ask each participating consumer to assemble pictures—either from original photographs taken by the participant or cut out from magazines—into a collage that expresses his or her thoughts and feelings about a product category or brand. Researchers then conduct an in-depth interview in which they use the collage as a stimulus to probe for the mental models driving the consumer's brand associations.[23] Although the technique is fairly time- and labor-intensive, for both researchers and consumer participants, many consumer-goods companies have

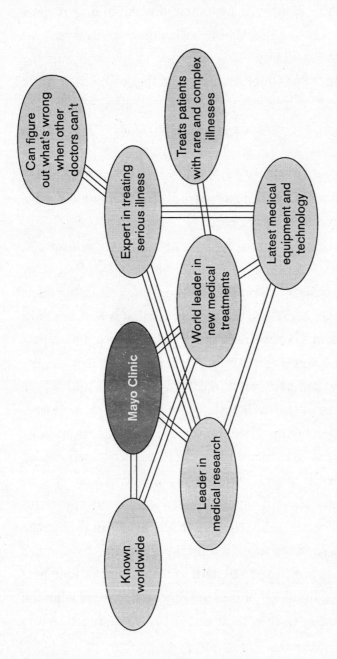

FIGURE 2. Brand Concept Map for Group Somewhat Unfamiliar with Mayo Clinic. *Source: Adapted from Deborah Roedder John et al. (2005), "Brand Concept Maps: A Methodology for Identifying Brand Association Networks," Cambridge, MA: Marketing Science Institute, Report No. 05-112, used with permission of the authors.*

found that the results deepen their understanding of how consumers perceive brands on both unconscious and conscious levels. For example, a "consensus" map combining the results of individual interviews showed that using the tagline "Like a Rock" in advertising for Chevy trucks evoked four basic linkages: the obvious one between "Chevy truck" and "rock," and also the less direct ones of "rock" and "take abuse"; "take abuse" with "reliable"; and "Chevy truck" with "reliable." The results thus suggested pathways for transferring desirable attributes onto the Chevy brand.[24]

Perceptual maps are useful in analyzing competition and market opportunities. With multidimensional scaling techniques, researchers can plot competitors on positioning maps where the axes represent the jugular attributes that are both very important to consumers and on which there is high perceived inter-brand competition. Managers can easily see the areas where competition is most concentrated and where there are gaps in the market that may present good opportunities for introducing a new product or line extension. Marketers can use the maps to understand how their brand compares with others within consumers' mental spaces, obtain a better sense of which connections are most powerful for consumers, and tailor their strategies accordingly. But the fact that these maps show the market from the consumer's perspective is both their strength and their limitation: consumers' thoughts about brands are more reflective of what the market is rather than what it might be—market innovators use such maps as valuable input, but radical innovation often comes from outside consumers' experiences.

From this grounding in, first, the connection between psychological associations with place and consumer desires and beliefs, and second, the connection between brands and mental spaces, we move in the next chapter to issues of managing physical place. A person's psychological associations and mental representations can create very strong expectations for what a product is and what it does, and how it is perceived in relation to other brands. These expectations and perceptions carry over into the retail experience and affect whether, how, how often, or for what purpose consumers frequent a store. Understanding these fundamentals, and using them to advantage, can drive higher patronage and sales.

Chapter 2

MANAGING PHYSICAL PLACE

In the Truman Capote novel *Breakfast at Tiffany's*, the lead character, Holly Golightly, perfectly describes the profound effect physical place has on us when she says:

> What I've found does the most good is just to get into a taxi and go to Tiffany's. It calms me down right away, the quietness and the proud look of it; nothing very bad could happen to you there, not with those kind men in their nice suits, and that lovely smell of silver and alligator wallets. If I could find a real-life-place that made me feel like Tiffany's, then I'd buy some furniture and give the cat a name.[1]

We may live in the digital age, but physical place still defines most purchasing behavior. Retail stores are where the vast

majority of sales to consumers are made; in the case of consumer packaged goods (products such as food and health and
beauty aids that are bought and sold frequently and generally
distributed through food and drug stores), fewer than 1 percent
of sales occur online.[2] Of the more than $150 billion worth of
clothing sold in the United States, less than 10 percent is bought
online. The online share of these and other categories may be
accelerating—both in America and Europe—but touch, sounds,
smells, and the social environment of brick-and-mortar shopping remain hugely important. Even the most sophisticated
online browsing systems cannot capture a shopper's attention
the same way a shirt on a display table or store shelf can.

How products are placed on store shelves, where those stores
are located, how inventory gets distributed to them, and even
how sales territories are assigned: these considerations have not
disappeared from the marketing mix. Quite the opposite. Busy
or distracted customers—which is to say, all customers—always
appreciate convenient location, good in-store design, and
shelves well stocked with the brands they favor (and that are
prominent in their mental maps). Companies that ignore those
realities forgo opportunities to excel around place. That simply
leaves a lot of money on the table, both in the form of additional
sales and more efficient operations.

There are many powerful examples of physical place decisions that have determined marketing success or failure. In
2007, United Kingdom retailer Tesco entered the U.S. market,
with the launch of the Fresh & Easy chain of neighborhood

markets in California. Fresh & Easy expanded rapidly in California, Arizona, and Nevada, gobbling up store locations abandoned by other retailers as well as new sites. But as of 2010, the 168 Fresh & Easy stores were collectively operating at a loss, leading Tesco to mothball 13 of them. Disappointing sales were attributed, in part, to poor community locations, where expected population growth never materialized. (Tesco's timing relative to the subprime-mortgage crisis and end of the housing boom could not have been worse.) Poor roadside locations were also at fault; many of the stores were convenient to turn into during the morning commute but inconvenient on the trip home, when consumers are ready to buy something for supper.[3]

Selecting store locations and determining the appropriate number and density of stores to meet demand are key physical place decisions. Mass-marketed products must be intensively distributed so as to be within an "arm's reach of desire" (as Coca-Cola management puts it), but more is not always better. Sometimes exclusive products that derive perceived value from scarcity, or that need point-of-sale service, should be distributed selectively.

Within a store, managing physical place can be critical to driving sales. The details of store layout and design, the flow of merchandise on offer, and the organization and appeal of shelf facings and displays all determine the perceived convenience of the shopping experience, the length of time spent in the store, and the average sales generated per visit.

Factory and distribution center locations are also important, in spite of trends in online buying. Michael Dell famously conceived a new market opportunity when he realized that a large percentage of consumers who were not first-time buyers of personal computers were confident enough to buy direct from the manufacturer, without in-store sales advice, especially if they were given a price incentive and online service support. Dell did not need to worry about store locations, but it did need to locate its factories and distribution centers in relation to the geographical distribution of consumer demand.

Together, the examples of Tesco and Dell illustrate the dynamism of the retail environment. Namely, that it is hard to get it right and it is hard to stay in contention when new ideas constantly challenge the status quo. In the 1950s, Malcolm McNair, a retailing expert at the Harvard Business School, used the term "revolving wheel of retailing" to describe a pattern in which a new form of retailing succeeds on the basis of lower prices and superior efficiency. But then those new retailers eventually add services and products, creating upward cost and price creep, which eliminates their competitive advantage and provides an umbrella for new low-cost forms of competition to enter. McNair's revolving wheel suggests constant opportunity and constant threat. The retailing environment is one in which new forms of competition continually arise in response to technological and consumer trends and competitive activity. In turn, these developments provide challenges and opportunities for manufacturers. For example, neighborhood grocery stores gave way to larger, more efficient, and lower cost supermarkets, which then left a niche for neighborhood convenience stores to satisfy consumers' needs for fast and easy fill-in shopping. At its inception, Snapple flourished by building up distribution in these smaller outlets rather than trying to crack the refrigerated sections of large supermarket chains. For both the convenience store and the Snapple brand, closely managing a small physical space defined their success.

Management Attention to Physical Location

In businesses today, the marketing function is nearly always split off from the sales and distribution functions, and the vast majority of consumer goods are sold through retailers rather than direct to consumers. This separation of marketing, sales, distribution, and retailing has contributed to the undervaluing of place in the marketing mix. It obscures the fact that, beginning with the first market stalls, a primary function of marketing has been to enable exchange by bringing goods, buyers, and sellers together in one physical location.

Until about the last half century, central roles for marketing management included management of the sales force and distribution systems—including, for example, selecting national and regional distributors, wholesalers, and retail chains. The sorting and matching processes in the sales and distribution systems allowed customers to find: the right products—the ones that fit their needs and desires—at the right stores—those that offered the right assortments, prices, shopping environment, etc.—at the right locations—places that were not too distant and conveniently accessible by car, bus, walking, or other mode of travel (see Figure 3). Complementing manufacturers' marketing activities, great merchandisers of the past possessed an intuitive grasp of the place and location factors that could trigger consumer purchases.

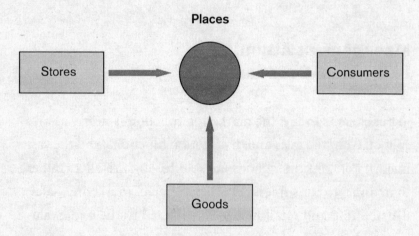

FIGURE 3. Marketing Matches Right Goods to Right Consumers to Right Stores at Right Places at Right Times

Sales, distribution, and marketing may now occupy their own functional silos, but place concerns all of them. Fitting together all the activities required to connect products and customers is just as important as ever. Cross-functional coordination can benefit from a greater appreciation of how place is central to management decisions—ranging from creating the appropriate in-store environment and stocking shelves to selecting retail locations, to logistics and shipping, to segmenting consumers and managing the sales force.

A good example of managing place decisions well is Apple, which, in 2007, *Fortune* magazine named as America's best retailer—somewhat surprising since the computer maker had opened its first store only six years previously, and many retailing experts had expected it to fail.[4] In addition to little retail experience, Apple accounted for a miniscule share of the personal computer market. Confounding predictions, by 2004, the stores were profitable. They reached $1 billion in annual sales faster than any other retailer in history; two years later, sales reached $1 billion a quarter. Part of this success is attributable to Apple's anticipation of the role the stores would play in showcasing the popular iPod product line, launched in fall 2001. The success may also be attributed to CEO Steve Jobs's intuitive merchandising brilliance and to rigorous planning and testing. When Jobs and executive Ron Johnson viewed a mock-up of the store they had originally designed, they were struck by the insight that "the hardware was laid out by product category—in other words, by how the company was organized internally, not by how a customer might actually want to buy things. . . . 'So we redesigned it,' [Jobs] says. 'And it cost us, I don't know, six, nine months. But it was the right decision by a million miles.'"[5] Thus, Apple stores have both "product zones" and "solution zones"—featuring, say, computers, cameras, and software matched to do digital photography. All Apple stores follow a set of standard specifications for arrangement of signage, tables, shelves, the "Genius Bar"—where tech-support staff are stationed to troubleshoot hardware and software issues—and placement of every object on the tables, from computers to power cords, to product information cards.

Shaping the Physical Environment for Shoppers

As soon as any of us enter a store, we respond consciously or unconsciously to the physical terrain—how it is laid out vertically and horizontally; and how aisles, shelves, and displays are positioned at the center and around the periphery. Some of this response is based on inherent human traits. Take these four: (1) people are attracted to sensory cues in the physical environment, such as color, fragrance, and the ability to touch; (2) we pay attention to things at eye level; (3) most people are right-handed and natural motion is to the right;[6] (4) we have a need to know our bearings and how to get from one space to another.

Accordingly, many supermarkets will position fresh produce front and center in waist- to eye-level display units to give a fresh and natural, upscale feel to a store. Other fresh foods are positioned along the store perimeter, to draw traffic around the store, while packaged goods dominate the interior aisles. Research shows that few shoppers travel the full length of all the interior aisles,[7] which is another reason for grocers to put meats and other fresh foods, which command higher profit margins, in primary circulation areas. Clothing retailers place tables near the front of the store stacked with colorful T-shirts and sweaters—often at special promotional prices—that can be touched and held and therefore draw shoppers in to engage with the merchandise. Likewise, grocery stores place colorful boxes of sugary cereals on lower shelves where children can easily see and reach them. Retailers engineer traffic flow, the directional bias of visual displays, and checkout counters and other points of interaction to suit right-hand dominance. They provide signage and floor plans to keep people from feeling lost, frustrated, and therefore less willing to spend, particularly in larger warehouse-size spaces. IKEA, whose spaces average a massive three hundred thousand square feet, sends consumers in a defined path throughout the store.

Many aspects of spatial design are intended to encourage people's tendencies to make unplanned or impulse purchases—those not put down in advance on mental or written shopping lists. For instance, IKEA's zigzag route passes areas stocked with inexpensive impulse-purchase items. For American consumers, under time pressure and for whom shopping is a routine, a large percentage—60 percent—of grocery store purchases are unplanned.[8] Similar percentages apply in other wealthy countries and for other types of stores. To spur impulse purchases, retailers station small-item purchase opportunities near the way in and the way out: for example, the cosmetics counters positioned near the first-floor entrances of department stores, or the candy displays at supermarket checkout stations. In addition to scattering low-price impulse items at hand level among the higher-priced furniture items in the main part of the store, IKEA also places a small-housewares section near the store exit. Items on end-aisle displays catch shoppers' attention and turn over significantly more quickly than items on regular shelves, even if not on sale (consumers often assume they are on sale).[9] Selling opportunities increase when aisles and displays are organized so that consumers visit more parts of the store and spend more minutes there. However, the navigational design of the physical space must steer a midcourse between shepherding shoppers and letting them loose, of tempting people without annoying them because they can't find what they need or because the shopping trip takes longer than expected.

Recently, in fact, retailers have been backing away from designing ever larger stores, prompted in large part by the multiyear recession. By reducing square footage, retailers are seeking to directly cut payrolls, rental and operating expenses, and inventory carrying costs. They're also seeking to avoid the desolate feel of large spaces with not enough customers or products to fill them. For their part, recession-battered consumers with lower discretionary incomes and lessened appetite for wandering around large-format stores appear to have welcomed the more focused merchandise selections and the ease of navigating a smaller store. A slimmed-down Anchor Blue clothing store in California, for example, improved profitability and foot traffic by cutting its square footage in half and paring inventory by about 15 percent.[10] Major big-box retailers such as Home Depot and Walmart are among those shifting their store mix toward smaller outlets. However, Walmart has found that for their core customers a certain amount of shelf and aisle clutter signals "bargain," while a too-pared-down appearance signals "expensive."[11]

For nonretailers, one point from these examples deserves particular attention: sales of a manufacturer's products are closely linked to where they appear in stores and how they are displayed. This necessitates active engagement with retailers to secure the most favorable locations.

Space Management

Shelf and floor space are limited and valuable commodities that expert retailers manage closely. In the grocery business, one way retailers maximize revenue per shelf is to charge manufacturers "slotting fees" to secure space for new items. The fees cover incremental costs of introducing new products, and more significantly, serve as insurance in case the new items prove to be duds that fail to generate sufficient profit per foot.

Given that shelf-space utilization is so critical, top suppliers in a category need to work hard to influence the design of retail planograms—diagrams that merchants use to specify exactly where and how many units of each brand, size, color, or style are to be placed. Retailers usually base these decisions on turnover rates, profit margins, package sizes, and item interactions (how placement of one item affects sales of another), but manufacturers can use their specialized knowledge of consumer behavior in their category to gain a positional advantage for their brands on the shelf. Manufacturers with sophisticated market research capabilities can also help merchandisers improve space allocation by analyzing data showing the effects of price promotions, displays, and cross-category affinities, such as which products are likely to be purchased together.[12]

In the mid-2000s, Campbell Soup Company achieved what it considers a breakthrough innovation in placing more than twenty thousand iQ Shelf Maximizer systems in grocery stores. The system, in which gravity feeds soup cans into fixed slots on shelf fixtures, increased sales by bringing order and discipline to shelves. Retailers benefited because Campbell paid for the system installation, created planograms and signage based on a particular store's sales and stocking data, and made space for store-brand soups. By making it easier for consumers to pick out their preferred variety and for store workers to keep shelves stocked, sales increased by more than 8 percent in participating stores. Subsequently, consumer research led to reorganizing soups by color-coded benefit categories—such as nutritious soups geared toward children— rather than by flavor. According to *Supermarket News*, "Campbell's research shows that when presented with a unit that's easier to shop, consumers will spend about 20 seconds, rather than 50, finding the soup they set out to buy. The time saved can then be used to browse additional varieties, creating an incremental sales opportunity."[13]

Two factors guiding the spatial arrangement of products into categories or clusters within a store are sales and operational efficiencies. Putting similar products near each other makes things convenient for salespeople and store personnel and also helps customers locate items. In some cases, grouping complementary items next to each other—such as hamburger meat, buns, and Heinz ketchup during a special promotion for summer barbecue season—increases sales by offering ready-made solutions to consumers' needs.

Manufacturers, of course, compete to be sure that their products are displayed to their best advantage. Retailers, on the other hand, seek to maximize the overall profit from all brands. Often they wish to locate their higher-unit-margin private-label products next to the equivalent national manufacturer brands, in direct competition. Some also believe that they need no more than three brand options—good, better, best—in any one category. So not all brands, and certainly not all stock-keeping units (SKUs) of any one brand make it onto the grocer's shelf. With net after-tax profit margins of just over 1 percent in U.S. grocery retailing, management must be ruthless about maximizing profit per linear foot of shelf space.

Competition for physical space does not stop at the shelf. The package itself is a battleground where a manufacturer's control of package space is compromised by such needs as regulatory requirements (for nutrition and potentially carbon-footprint labeling) and labels or other marks required by "ingredient brands" included in the product (such as "made with NutraSweet" or "Intel Inside").

Store Traffic Measurement

Like many retailers and other institutions that serve the public, Apple stores use high-tech video systems to measure and analyze customer traffic.[14] Cash-register receipts record customer purchases. Traffic data record how many shoppers enter the store and possibly where customers go within the store, thus allowing calculation of the "curiosity factor" of consumer interest and the conversion rate of lookers into buyers.

Increasingly, the new tracking systems feed into marketing programs where what a consumer sees in terms of in-store ads or promotional offers depends on his or her movements. Based on store traffic data, retailers can target ads to the aisles where consumers are most likely to be at specific times of day. Developers are working on shopping carts equipped with sensors that trigger a relevant ad on a cart-mounted display or on a nearby LED display when a customer pauses at a particular spot. So when a shopper stops in the laundry-detergent aisle, he or she may suddenly be greeted with an ad for Tide. Or when one picks up a particular detergent brand, a device may generate a coupon for the same manufacturer's—or a competitor's— fabric softener.[15] In another variation, currently being tested by Second Generation and Tyson, shoppers can scan a product with their smartphone and receive points, coupons, or even games in return.[16]

Facial recognition software in tracking systems can tell whether people are old or young, male or female.[17] In casinos, surveillance systems and loyalty/payment cards track when players enter or leave the gaming areas and which tables or slots they go to. It's almost as though retailing is becoming a video-game form of reality where shoppers are the game pieces. This level of surveillance raises obvious privacy concerns, particularly if consumers have no opportunity to opt in or opt out. But on the plus side to consumers, the results may include better-targeted promotional offers, greater efficiency in marketing expenditures, and, ultimately, lower prices.

Locating Retail Outlets

An entertaining and highly popular guide to business success, published in 1916, related the tale of the eponymous advertising executive Obvious Adams, who investigated the root causes of a failure of a department store's advertising campaign to boost sales. By observing pedestrian traffic around the store, Adams realized that despite the store's Main Street address, its frontage on the street was poor, so shoppers failed to notice it—a problem advertising could not fix. Instead, he advised the store to relocate as soon as its lease expired.[18]

The familiar real-estate maxim "location, location, location" applies to marketers just as much as to home buyers. Some locations seem doomed from the start, where store after store fails to make a go of it. Retailers obviously want to avoid these ill-starred sites, but more subtle mismatches of store and location can occur as well. If the location decision doesn't fit the overall business strategy, isn't a good fit with the needs or habits of local customers, or ignores the impact of other retailers, the odds of success plummet. Similarly, manufacturers with a selective, rather than mass-market, distribution strategy will want to evaluate retailers on these criteria.

Location decisions include considerations on breadth and depth of geographical coverage; selection of metro areas, towns, and cities; and adding, moving, reformatting, or deleting facilities from the store portfolio. Nike, for instance, recently unveiled a five-year plan to add between 250 and 300 stores worldwide to its existing portfolio of 450 stores. Nike's very first locations were the enormous, splashy Niketown theme-park-style stores in large, urban downtown centers. In contrast, the new portfolio will add smaller-scale stores, ranging from about three thousand to six thousand square feet, carrying assortments tailored to sports interests of local customers—such as a running-products store in Palo Alto, California, and a soccer-products store in Manchester, England (an instance of market segmentation based on physical location plus attitudes and interests). Somewhat larger "brand experience" stores will replicate aspects of Niketowns,[19] but both types of stores are designed so that fixtures can be rearranged almost overnight. Thus, the new location strategy and store design reflect a desire to streamline the shopping experience for customers and to build more flexibility into retail operations. This approach fits the reality of the new consumer psychology, where people are exhibiting a desire to simplify consumption.[20] It also supports the company's growth strategy by allowing it to adjust quickly to local conditions as it tests the waters in new markets.

Regarding individual store location, take a few of the issues Steve Jobs considered when deciding where to locate the first Apple stores. Apple wanted both to showcase the brand and to sell significant numbers of products—in contrast to the Nike-town brand showcase stores, where overhead costs often out-stripped sales. This strategy required placing the stores in metropolitan areas with high concentrations of adventure-some consumer-technology buyers. But exactly where? As recounted in *Fortune*, the real-estate strategy was what "Jobs calls 'Ambush the customer.' He says he wanted to show Win-dows users 'how much better a Mac is. But Windows users weren't going to drive to a destination.' That's why [Apple retail head Ron] Johnson waited so long for the San Francisco location—a corner off Market Street where people live, work, shop, tour, and play, as he puts it. 'The real estate was a lot more expensive,' says Jobs, but it was worth it because people 'didn't have to gamble with 20 minutes of their time. They only had to gamble with 20 footsteps of their time.'"[21] Since then, Apple has continued to locate its stores in high-traffic areas. As of 2010, operating income, or profits, from retail operations were $2.4 billion, and average revenue per store was a healthy $34.1 million.[22]

Store location decisions typically involve a complex mix of inputs (see Figure 4). Retailers have traditionally depended on personal observation, rules of thumb, and instinct to guide their location decisions.[23] There are also quantitative models to assist in selecting countries, regions, cities, and particular sites. For example, "gravity models"—based on the relative population size and distance apart of places—have been used to define the probability that a customer will patronize one of two or more retailing centers in a particular metropolitan

Company and corporate marketing strategy

Locational strategy:

- Territorial coverage

- Depth of penetration of market areas

- Locations within market areas best matched with target customers

Decision inputs:

- Managerial experience, e.g., observation, intuition, rules of thumb, and analogies

- Models and analytical techniques, e.g., centrality models, gravitational models, expert systems, statistical data analysis

- Quantitative data mapped to geography, e.g., census, GIS, customer and competitor characteristics, cost/ft^2

Store portfolio decisions:

- Rollout of new stores

- Relocation of existing stores to different shopping centers, etc.

- Reformatting of stores

- Closures of stores

FIGURE 4. Elements of Retail Locational Decision Making

area. The results could be depicted as contour maps of each center's market area. In general, the centrality and gravity models work less well at the scale of individual shopping centers than at the wider town, city, or regional scale.[24] Also in modern urban environments, distance is an oversimplification: it fails to take into account travel time and traffic flows, and it may not be a strong determinant of consumer choice for relatively short distances.[25]

With the advent of computers and advanced data collection capabilities, location specialists can increasingly calculate optimal store-location decisions based on additional factors and more precise data. These include rents and occupancy costs and projected sales, in addition to geo-demographic factors, such as size and density of trading areas, age and income levels, and transportation modes. Similar to the monitoring of in-store consumer shopping behavior, tracking services observe and measure shopping patterns and traffic between stores within shopping centers. The new geographical information systems (GIS) permit more detailed mapping of these types of data.

Although the formal quantitative approaches are becoming cheaper and more widely available, retailers continue to rely heavily on the experiential or "artistic" bases for judgment.[26] As retail competition has intensified, perhaps the most important goal for marketers has been to gain a more precise and complete understanding of the psychological factors that motivate people to visit a particular shopping location. For example, because shoppers seek to minimize travel distance, inconvenience, and time, that may mean stopping at a grocery store that is on the same side of the street they're on as they travel home from work. (As mentioned earlier, Tesco reportedly failed to take this factor into account.) Or it could mean that a shopper chooses to visit a location with wider parking spaces. For routine purchases of common products like soft drinks or snacks, these may be the deciding factors.

In some instances, it is the wide assemblage of products that motivates consumers to travel to a destination. Hence, supermarkets of one hundred thousand square feet, in which consumers can complete a full range of shopping errands, draw customers from a much wider area than a neighborhood convenience store of three thousand square feet. Big-box retailers (such as discount stores like Walmart or Target), off-price stores (such as Marshall's), warehouse clubs (like Costco), and category specialists (such as Home Depot or Best Buy) can offer a combination of low or moderate prices and wide selection that may justify a special trip to a more distant location. Or consumers may be in the market for something like a piece of furniture, but they don't know exactly what brand or style they want; and so they would like to browse a wide selection, either from a mega furniture store or a cluster of stores.

In other words, retailers and manufacturer brands are part of an ecosystem where the vast majority share symbiotic locational relationships with other retailers and brands, even direct competitors. Fast-food chains located near each other help draw a critical mass of shoppers that benefits all. Informally, groups of street vendors in Washington DC, selling the same product also congregate in the same area. One aspect of the Walmart strategy—to pick off smaller towns that only have enough buying power for one such store—would seem to be an exception. But even in the case of big-box stores located on isolated sites, over time, other retailers tend to cluster around them.

The Apple brand exerts a powerful pull on consumers' imaginations, and Apple stores might be thought of as "destination stores" strong enough to attract customers in their own right. Nevertheless, for Apple and most other manufacturer or retailer brands, there remains safety in numbers—whether in a downtown area; along a commercial street or in a strip mall; in a midsize or large regional shopping center; or among a cluster of stores appealing to the same customers or carrying similar merchandise or featuring the same lifestyle, such as an "automotive mile," or a Fifth Avenue or Champs-Elysées. As Apple expanded into urban and suburban malls, it tended to set up shop alongside stores like Pottery Barn, Williams-Sonoma, and J.Crew that also attracted design-conscious, less price-sensitive types of customers.

Delivering Physical Products

Distribution may not be the glamorous part of marketing, but it's essential. Wherever stores are located, they must have dependable access to supplies of goods. Western consumers take for granted an abundance of fresh produce, meat, and dairy in supermarkets stocked with fifty thousand or more

SKUs. Local mall stores feature shelf after shelf and rack after rack of fast-moving consumer goods, plus shoes, clothing, electronics, household items, and much more. The goal of some manufacturers is to be within reach wherever consumer desire strikes. Supply systems in general operate effectively, linking multiple points, but manufacturers, retailers, and shippers must keep up as competitors continue to raise the bar. UPS and other delivery companies meticulously plan delivery routes to minimize time- and gas-consuming left turns for their trucks. Walmart, in particular, has thrived by wringing inefficiencies out of the supply chains, often leaning heavily on suppliers like Procter & Gamble.

Distribution must also be responsive to local variations in demand. Big retailers like Target operate with a platform of common products, then add on products to suit local or regional specialized tastes. Ford and General Motors (GM) dealers know that the mix of vehicles needed on dealer lots varies widely by geographic region and by time of year. A Ford dealer in Maine, for instance, will carry a higher percentage of rugged F-150 pickup trucks in its vehicle inventory; while a Ford dealer in Boston will carry a higher percentage of sedans, but stock up on four-wheel drive vehicles before the onset of winter. Optimizing the locations of sources of supply and of distribution centers grows more complex as the number of local variants increases. To reduce the number of distribution points involved and to maximize control, some manufacturers operate their own distribution systems. Both Coca-Cola and PepsiCo have acquired independent bottlers to consolidate, build scale, and achieve cost efficiencies in core geographies.

The key point, too easily slighted in the thick of operations, is that distribution strategy must go hand in hand with marketing strategy. Whether the strategy is to reach a mass market or a niche market, distribution must support it. For example, beer is a perishable product, and, because of its low bulk-to-value ratio, an expensive one to truck. So mass-marketer ABInBev, the result of the merger between Anheuser-Busch and Belgium's InBev, operates a dozen breweries located at strategic points around the United States, where it has access to both quality raw ingredients and to consumer markets. A network of independent beer wholesalers and company-owned wholesale operations constitutes the most extensive distribution system in the industry, reaching more than 450,000 retail locations. Indeed, the press release announcing the merger of the two beverage giants cited Anheuser-Busch's "world-class sales and distribution system" along with "the successful U.S. distribution partnership for InBev's European import brands" and the "complementary footprint" of the two companies internationally as strong foundations for future growth.[27] The system is not available to the niche-market microbreweries, which, in contrast, move through a more patchwork system of reseller companies and more than a thousand often overlapping disorganized distributors. For a successful microbrewery wanting to grow to the next level, cracking the distribution system is a much greater challenge than advertising or product development.

Distribution was also a key factor in the growth strategy of the Snapple family of fruit-based drinks. In the 1990s, Snapple demand grew apace in the New York area, where the company was founded, fueled by consumer desire for unique, natural-ingredient alternatives to carbonated beverages. In the United States, early demand for new consumer products typically occurs on the west and east coasts and, from there, spreads to the middle of the country. A hit product on one coast will typically spark demand quickly on the other coast. However, Snapple's glass bottles were expensive to ship cross-country, and Snapple could not establish new manufacturing fast enough to meet demand in the west. Wisely, Snapple held back its distribution development west of the Mississippi to increase its scarcity value and consolidate its position in the east. That is, by being unavailable west of the Mississippi, Snapple stoked demand in the east because consumers associated the product with exclusivity—something their friends in the west wanted but could not get hold of. Distribution went national only later.

Out-of-Stocks Are Not Trivial

Whether supply systems are a simple step straight from a local production plant or are a multilayered chain involving two or more levels of distributors spanning continents, a series of small inefficiencies in the system can add costs and impede sales if items go out of stock at the end of the channel. In supermarkets and other stores selling fast-moving consumer goods, approximately 8 to 10 percent of the SKUs are out of stock at any given time.[28] A review for the supermarket industry found that, worldwide, when an item was out of stock, close to a third of shoppers went to another store to buy it. Out-of-stocks are a major concern for manufacturers as well: while some shoppers switched to another SKU from the same brand, a quarter of them elected to buy another brand instead, and 9 percent made no purchase at all.[29] In the United States, lost grocery sales resulting from out-of-stocks were estimated to equate to 3 percent of annual sales—a serious loss given the tight margins in the grocery industry.[30]

Clothing manufacturer Hugo Boss AG reaped substantial gains from improving product availability. Its average in-stock rate on SKUs of bodywear was an already high 98.24 percent but this average masked periods when in-stocks of the most popular styles dropped to about 85 percent. Boosting the in-stock rate to 99.96 percent reportedly increased sales by 32 percent in part because retailers removed substitute, or "insurance," brands from their product lineups, which they had carried to cover the periods of inadequate stock.[31] Of course the flip side of the problem, overstocking, can result in excess inventories at the end of the fashion season and mark-downs on obsolete merchandise.

Good distribution systems must be able to handle both predictable and unpredictable fluctuations in demand. According to the Grocery Manufacturers of America, "out-of-stock rates nearly double during store promotions, jumping from 7.4 percent out-of-stock to 13.1 percent out-of-stock."[32] One advantage of an "everyday low pricing" strategy, whereby retailers reduce the number of promotional events and even out the temporary cuts in their retail prices over time, is that it lowers fluctuations in consumer demand and hence lowers distribution costs. But, in some cases, demand is simply not even. Vicks closely monitors weather trends to predict where demand for cold remedies will spike in the United States, and it boosts inventories and pays supermarkets allowances for end-aisle displays to meet demand in high flu areas. To a certain extent, Vicks can prepare in advance, but nimble distribution on short notice is a key element in its strategy.

Tracking Product Locations

Knowing where products are physically located—on retail shelves, in warehouses, in transit—is a cornerstone of inventory management. Despite technological advances, all the potential gains from better tracking of product movements have yet to be achieved. Shoppers are familiar with the UPC bar codes retailers use to scan items at checkout and update their inventory lists. UPC scanners are manually operated, but the newer technology of radio frequency identification (RFID) wirelessly transmits data from a microchip tag attached to a pallet or case or an item to an automatic reader; it's basically the same technology used by New York state's E-ZPass system to collect tolls from responders mounted on car windshields.

Although RFID has been around for more than a decade, and provides greatly improved tracking of product movements, it has still not been fully adopted in distribution channels, primarily because of cost concerns. The expense of installing readers, tags that cost a dollar or more each, upfront software integration, and changes to business processes all add up to a significant investment. In addition to start-up costs, there also exist concerns about the reliability of the technology and whether manufacturers and retailers in general, or in specific cases, would gain equally. On the benefit side, where RFID has been implemented, there are fewer out-of-stocks, better just-in-time inventory, reduced distribution-center costs, and lower rates of "shrinkage"—that is, missing or stolen items.[33] The industry has succeeded in reducing the cost of tags to the range of twenty to forty cents apiece and is aiming for a five-cent tag. If that happens and is followed by more universal adoption, global marketers will be able to track precisely where a product is in the distribution chain at any point in time. To reiterate the importance of cross-functional and channel-member cooperation, turning this capability into a responsive distribution system that quickly puts products in the right places to meet consumer demand requires more than data: it requires close coordination among manufacturers, distributors, and retailers.

Burgeoning Consumer Interest in Product Sourcing and Delivery

Distribution chains are largely invisible to consumers and historically have been of little concern. All that is changing. Thanks to the growing environmental movement, consumers are increasingly conscious of where products come from, the distances they must travel, and the modes of transportation used to get them to their destination. More and more consumers view organic, local produce as a healthier alternative and as a way of helping their own communities. In Great Britain, it's increasingly common to see the carbon costs of supermarket items on display, as national retailers like Tesco press their private-label and branded goods suppliers to provide more information. As part of a two-pronged effort to reduce its direct carbon emissions and to help consumers make green choices, Tesco has so far placed carbon-footprint information on a hundred of its own-brand products. Taking into account raw ingredients, the manufacturing process, packaging, distribution and retailing, and consumer use and disposal of an empty bottle or can, Coca-Cola, for instance, has calculated that the carbon footprint of a 330 milliliter can of regular Coke is 170 grams versus 150 grams for the same-sized can of Diet Coke; or 360 grams for a 330 milliliter glass bottle of regular Coke.[34] Although it is not yet known precisely to what extent such information affects consumer choices, manufacturers including Walkers and Quaker Oats are betting they will be recognized and rewarded for being in the forefront of labeling their carbon footprint and taking steps to reduce it.

Carbon footprinting and environmental concerns imply that managers may have to reassess supply chains that were optimized around cheap shipping costs (which benefited from a surplus of container-ship capacity and intense competition among UPS, DHL and FedEx for express delivery business around the world). If you add the carbon footprint calculation, long supply chains become less attractive (leaving aside the freshness implications for perishables or consumer interest in patronizing local producers).

The opportunity costs of not responding in a timely fashion to customer demand—plus the rising wages of overseas labor and increases in shipping costs; plus costs such as those associated with correcting quality problems, theft of intellectual property, and piracy on the high seas—can indicate that a return to manufacturing based in the United States or neighboring Mexico is newly feasible for high-bulk, high-value-added products. NCR is switching the manufacture of ATMs sold in the United States to a new plant in Georgia in order to facilitate supplier and customer input into new product development. Shorter supply chains may become increasingly attractive on a total cost (including environmental) basis.

The case for reducing geographic distances from producers to consumers is buttressed by a recent spate of quality problems in consumer products, including: adulterated milk; tainted pet food; lead-painted children's toys from China; salmonella in eggs from Iowa and peanut butter from Georgia; and overheating laptop computer batteries from Asian manufacturing plants. When production of products is consolidated in just a few places, and massive distribution systems send those products all over the country or all over the world, to be sold under different brand names (twenty-four brand names in the case of one Iowa egg producer), a quality problem at one source quickly becomes a universal problem. Unwinding those distribution chains to trace the paths of defective products turns out to be incredibly difficult and time-consuming.[35]

From Mass to Localized Marketing

In the United States, the 1950s through the 1970s saw huge growth in national-scale marketing. Although the antitrust cases against A&P in the 1930s inhibited the spread of vertically integrated national supermarket chains—until the weakening of antitrust regulation and enforcement during the Reagan administration—national brands and national marketers thrived, aided by the ascension of both the national postal service (which facilitated direct mail ordering) and national television advertising. It was an era where marketers encouraged every family in every part of the country to aspire to consume the same products and brands.

During the 1980s, as we noted in the introduction, national brands increasingly adapted their products and marketing programs to the preferences of different market segments. One reason they did so was that as mass markets became saturated and competition intensified, differentiating or customizing one or more elements of the marketing program was a path toward higher prices and higher profits. When preferences clustered into discrete geographical areas, local marketing was a convenient form of market segmentation. Plus, local advertising media were typically more cost efficient than national advertising. For example, carmakers emphasized different models in their advertising depending on regional tastes.

A second factor favoring localized marketing by national brands was the growing power of retailers and distributors and their ability to demand differentiated programs customized to local markets. A third important force abetting localization was the advent of store scanner data, which gave marketers more precise feedback on how well products and marketing programs fared in different geographies, retailing chains, and individual stores. After store club cards were introduced, marketers could tell not just which products were sold that day, or which products were bought together, but also which products an individual customer habitually bought.

Localized marketing could be dictated by a variety of distinctive local conditions that made a one-size-fits-all strategy inappropriate. These might be inescapable physical conditions. Hard water in Europe meant that soap didn't lather well and left a film around the bathtub. This spawned the emergence of shower gels that provided as much lather in the shower as bath foams did in the tub. Or the conditions could be ingrained or acquired preferences. Thus, national brands of coffee changed their blends from one region to another. Or the conditions might be cultural or competitive. H-E-B is a highly successful Texas supermarket chain that adroitly adjusts its assortment to fit the tastes of a more heavily Hispanic consumer base that occupies some areas.

Nowadays, for many marketers, there is no turning away from localization. On the retailing side, former longtime Tesco CEO, Terry Leahy, says that to win in the grocery industry, you have to become the best local retailer. That means tailoring product assortments to each store. It also means tailoring store type to neighborhood. In the heart of London, for example, the smaller-size Tesco Metro stores cater to commuters or urban dwellers.

For some retailers, localization is a healthy retreat from a tilt too far toward standardization and centralization. Over the past few decades, the department store industry, for example, experienced waves of mergers and consolidations, in which regional stores or chains with distinct identities—such as Marshall Field's in Chicago, or Rich's in Atlanta—were swallowed up by ever-larger chains, eventually ending up under the ownership of the number one chain, Federated. When Federated changed its name to Macy's in 2007 and rebranded many of the acquisitions under the same name, centralization for the sake of efficiency seemed to have won the day. However, as sales slipped, Macy's soon conceded that it needed to tailor assortments and services to suit local preferences. Under the "My Macy's" rubric, the company restructured from four into three geographical units, but created new district and regional manager positions to oversee local stores, and emphasized the gathering of detailed information about local customers, for example by requiring merchandise buyers to visit stores daily and collecting observations from store managers and sales clerks. Despite a down period for most retailers, in the first year of localization, Macy's operating income increased.

On the national manufacturer side, three types of products are especially conducive to local marketing: (1) those where there are local differences in consumer behavior, trade, or competitive position; (2) those based on mature technologies with few functional quality differences relative to each other and to store brands, in which case, locally tailored sales promotions can increase market share; and (3) those where there is less potential for cross-market diversion if offered at different prices in different markets (such as high bulk-to-value products like pasta versus high value-to-bulk products like health and beauty aids). Strong franchise brands are also good candidates for local marketing—both because franchisees are usually local businessmen, and the businesses in combination such as a regional group of Ford or General Motors car dealers can generate enough sales volume to fund local advertising programs.

Some degree of localization is nearly always advisable, but must be planned carefully. As with all segmentation schemes, program costs and administrative complexity increase with localized marketing. Some companies overdo localization. For example, consumer goods companies often run different levels of price promotion on the same product in neighboring cities and states, based on differences in the product's market share. If the price differences are too great, the cross-market diversion mentioned above occurs. In other words, distributors in the lower-price city may buy and resell product to distributors in the higher-price city, especially if the bulk-to-value ratio is low enough to absorb the extra transportation costs. In addition, temporary promotions reduce the predictability of demand and manufacturing efficiency, resulting in either out-of-stocks and lost sales or the need for extra buffer inventories, which increases working capital costs.

In order to justify the apparent benefits stemming from customization (in terms of higher unit margins and/or higher customer penetration), you must more than offset the incremental costs. Moreover, you run the risk that excessive local marketing may dilute the brand franchise if your brand positioning and messages are inconsistent—especially in cases where consumers are likely to buy or pay attention to the product category as they travel around different areas. If the field salespeople who execute local marketing are compensated on short-term sales, then they may tend to cut deals that undermine long-term growth and profitability. Furthermore, having many different products and programs for many local markets requires greater management time and effort, and may direct resources away from strategically important issues—such as a focus on true innovation.

Historically, as localized marketing gathered steam, it raised complicated issues of how much responsibility to give to local managers. Among national companies, brand managements typically were centralized and nationally focused, whereas sales forces were often organized into local sales territories. Some firms elected to make all decisions at the national level, with minimal discretion given to the local salesperson. Others centralized planning and budgets but, in addition to a national plan, delegated a portion of the promotion budget to district and regional sales managers, who could use it at their discretion to maximize support from local distributors and retailers. In individual firms, the pendulum often swung back and forth as top management changed or as neither solution seemed optimal.

Currently, because local merchandising effectiveness increasingly depends on fine-grained data and analyses residing in centralized information systems, there may be reduced need for local sales force management autonomy. Anheuser-Busch, for instance, centralized store-level planning that had previously been decentralized. In the new system, field wholesaler reps continued to play a vital role in implementation: they were responsible for collecting shelf-status information via handheld, wireless tablet computers and also for implementing shelf plans, customized down to the store level.[36] Of course, the degree of local sales force autonomy will depend on the nature of the business and what creates most value for the customer. For example, mobile technology empowered independent financial advisers selling insurance products from French insurer Generali by enabling them to download client-specific information while visiting customers at their home or place of business.[37]

Sales Force Territories

A perennial issue in sales management is simply how to assign customer accounts to salespeople in the best way possible. Dating back to the days when the primary mode of communication with customers was face-to-face and most customers could be called on in a single location, territories for salespeople and distributors were assigned geographically. Usually companies attempted to draw boundaries so as to equalize distance traveled, workloads, actual or potential revenues, current customers, good prospects, and so forth.

To this day, location is a key factor in territory assignments, but there are numerous variations on geographical sales force assignments (see Figure 5). Sales force resources can be assigned by geography alone, by size of account, and/or by product or customer industry. Organizing by geography alone is especially appropriate when a company's target market comprises a large number of locally based customers in a variety of different industries. But many corporate accounts have facilities dispersed across the map; corporate management may allow local managers to procure certain categories of supplies from local vendors, while, for other categories, they will enforce a national procurement agreement. Thus, the selling company may assign one or more experienced reps to handle all sales to large, national customer accounts that span geographical territories. The result is a hybrid structure of national accounts for large customers and geographic territories for small customers. In this case, salespeople in the relevant geographical territories may be asked to check on order fulfillment and to provide support services. If customer support responsibilities do overlap between the local and national groups, this structure can create internal coordination problems and tricky compensation issues.

In other situations, when a company sells many different types of products in high enough volumes, each product line or business unit may have its own sales force and territorial structure. This creates another coordination problem, when several salespeople representing different divisions of the same company are calling on the same customers. Another variant occurs when customer requirements for products vary significantly. Firms may then assign groups of salespeople by customer and/or product type in districts that are not always geographically contiguous.

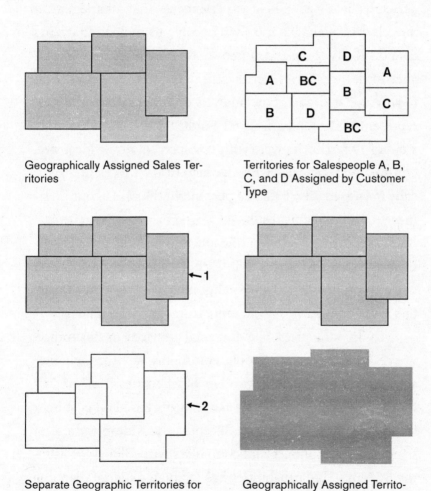

Geographically Assigned Sales Territories

Territories for Salespeople A, B, C, and D Assigned by Customer Type

Separate Geographic Territories for Product Line 1 and Product Line 2

Geographically Assigned Territories plus National Account

FIGURE 5. Examples of Sales Territories

Sales force allocation experts Andris Zoltners and Prabhakant Sinha say that well-crafted territory design can produce higher sales, reduce travel time and other costs, boost morale, and promote fair compensation and other rewards. In practice, they found that sales force territories were rarely perfectly balanced. Their experience is that mathematical models are invaluable in solving problems such as analyzing data on thirty thousand zip codes to draw five hundred balanced sales territories, or for redrawing territories based on freshly updated data. One analysis of 4,800 sales territories, representing 18 companies and 4 industries, showed that only 4 out of 10 territories were within 15 percent of the ideal size. Optimizing territories with the help of data modeling typically increased sales by 2 to 7 percent; in the case of one pharmaceutical company, results improved by about 50 percent.[38] But, in reporting a number of applications in the pharmaceutical industry, they stress that territory alignment works best when recommendations from alignment experts at headquarters are combined with local input from field sales managers.[39]

Even in industries like financial services or insurance, where brokers or salespeople commonly sift through networks of acquaintances regardless of where prospects or customers are located, updating assignments based on customer location remains important. Recently, the widespread use of handheld smartphones and computers with Global Positioning System (GPS) capabilities has facilitated digital mapping of districts and salespeople. In some of the more complex schemes, a team of salespeople with different specialties may be assigned to each account, but each of these people may have a different territory. Thus, a lead salesman may handle twenty accounts in one metropolitan area while a technical specialist may rotate among thirty accounts across two cities. With digital maps and GPS pinpointing, managers can easily recalibrate territories for each salesperson, or see where each member of a team is at any point in time.

Linking Physical and Psychological Place

Whether it's a matter of designing store layouts, figuring out where to locate retail facilities, localizing marketing, or aligning sales force territories, the best marketers combine quantitative analysis and modeling with more qualitative insights into the human responses to physical places. The physical landscape, the buildings, the relation to surrounding places, and how people perceive and behave all contribute to the gestalt of a particular place.

Think of the variety of restaurants and the different needs satisfied by marketing decisions concerning place. An Italian restaurant in the heart of Greenwich Village in New York offers an experience distinctly different from an Olive Garden in a suburban mall, despite similarities in menu offerings. One is subtly more authentic to an Old World experience, the other more reassuring of conformity to the tastes of an average American family. Or think of how Apple stores changed the experience of purchasing electronic products by creating a sleek, aesthetically appealing retail environment where all elements harmonize with product designs and subtly encourage the consumer to sample all the devices on display. In contrast, big-box computer retailers treat the products more like commodities and offer fewer opportunities for trying them out.

Sorting out the relationships between place and experience is not always straightforward or simple. For one thing, the actual unfolding of the experience affects the essence of the thing being experienced. For a couple of decades, Starbucks was able to move beyond its Seattle roots to export its "third place" and fine-coffee experience across the United States and internationally. Consumers sought out the coffee shops because they perceived them as special and unique. But as the chain expanded, these qualities were diluted and the stores seemed cookie-cutter as well as ubiquitous. As the company started to experiment with new formats and unbranded stores, Schultz acknowledged that "Today, because of the size and scale and ubiquity of the company, it's more important for us to demonstrate local relevance and a higher respect for local communities."[40]

Starbucks faces the same challenge that many successful, fast-growth brands face: how to stay true to your local roots, your company heritage, and the early adopting consumers who brought you to the dance. Every Starbucks has its own mix of customers: some have a sizable grab-and-go contingent, others a large number of patrons who seek a relaxing place to linger and socialize. And the rhythm of business varies as well: some stores are packed solid at commuting times; others draw a large morning crowd; others find students are their main customers in late afternoon on their way home from schools. Individual stores can succeed only when their managers are given the freedom to adapt assortments and assign store labor to match the local business opportunity. Starbucks can afford the costs of adaptation and, given Starbucks' prices, customers have a right to expect considerable local tailoring of the product and service offer.

Success for companies hoping to effectively unite psychological space associations with physical realities may require probing beneath expressed consumer sentiments. Some consumers may profess that the true neighborhood porch is the local coffee shop put out of business by Starbucks or that the true civic boosters are the local butchers, hardware stores, and banks put out of business by mammoth corporations that source products overseas instead of domestically. Despite such sentiments, many still flock to Starbucks and the big-box chain stores because they offer broad assortments of competitive brands at attractive prices.

Great brands, in short, find ways to use physical space to optimize positive consumer associations and sales success. In the next chapter, we discuss how marketers face the same challenges in using virtual space.

Chapter 3

MANAGING VIRTUAL PLACE

For years, pundits have said that e-commerce presages the death of distance and the demise of place in modern marketing. Nothing could be further from the truth. Even as more and more people go online, they still tend to seek out information, connections, and activities that are close to them. They read news related to their community or country, participate in social networks comprised of friends and family, and buy from local and domestic retailers.

Virtual place has gained dominance over physical place in very few goods and services categories when it comes to the selling process. Software, music, telecommunications, and financial services show the highest percentage of virtual sales because they require no movement of physical product. Yet despite the increase in digital product sales, the music industry, one of the hardest hit in the shift away from physical goods, continued to earn half its revenues, through 2010, on physical products sales. Though sales of e-books are accelerating, online booksellers like Amazon still deliver more printed books than e-books. All told, in 2010 e-book revenues in the United States amounted to $441.3 million, or under 4 percent of total book sales of $11.67 billion.[1] True, online bookstores can offer enormous choice, but they coexist alongside the local bookstore with its easy browsing, instantly available merchandise, like-minded customers, knowledgeable store personnel, and pleasant ambience.

And even as online retailers and e-products gain popularity, marketers must realize that the rules of managing physical space still apply in the virtual world. Purely online firms have no physical environments in which they engage with customers, so it is especially vital that the look and feel of a Web site conform to consumers' needs so they can find the content they're seeking and assess the trustworthiness of the marketer. Intuitive search and easy, convenient fulfillment boost consumers' confidence. Orbitz, for example, has done a good job of allowing consumers to search among a wide range of trip scenarios and providing price transparency before checkout.

For many marketers, virtual space complements rather than completely replaces physical space. Out of the hundreds of millions of Google queries per day, one out of five searches is related to location.[2] Millions of people use search engines to find the physical locations of businesses, or to compare the price, features, and reviews of different products in a category before going to the store to complete the purchase. These searches increasingly happen on the go, as smartphones connect businesses and consumers on the fourth screen (after television, personal computer, and laptop). Marketers can now send messages to individual phones based on their real-time location— meaning that a neighborhood restaurant, for example, can target people passing within a hundred yards of its front door during the lunch hour. Such applications promise to boost further the low-cost local marketing trend that Google began when local retailers could advertise around Google searches on keywords rather than relying on classified advertising in local newspapers.

While the enabling conditions for a wave of "hyperlocal" advertising from consumer goods marketers are not quite in place, within a couple of years they will be. The ability to target consumers in a specific physical place at any given time via the virtual places of their mobile phones will vastly improve the efficiency and effectiveness of marketing messaging. For their part, with interactive mobile devices, consumers effectively will be able to say to marketers, "This is what I want and need at this particular time and place." Wherever one goes, a personal marketplace of one will go too.

Consumers' Usage of Virtual Space

As of 2009, about one-quarter of the world's population, or 1.73 billion people, used the Internet at least once a month. Of the multitude of reasons people go online, many are driven by consumption—searching for information relevant to shopping or to purchase products or services directly. Increasingly, consumers go online to participate in social networks, which serve as sources of product information, including word of mouth and advertising.[3]

One open question is whether any particular mode of buying—offline or online—can provide all the elements desired by consumers in the purchase experience. Every channel has strengths and weaknesses. Relevant things to consider include the presence or absence of visual and tactile information; the level of trust people have in the business; choice; ease of purchase; interactivity; and an engaging environment (see Figure 6). While online shopping is generally more effective in providing information, choice, and convenience, the jury is out on lower prices and price transparency (especially when shipping and handling charges are added just before checkout). The most significant gaps may be in customer service and the social or physical environment of a good retail store. At the end of the day, even as customers move online, the retailers that will succeed in getting their attention and repeat business are the ones that can offer these same advantages as the old-fashioned real-world shop.

E-Shopping plus Traditional Shopping

According to a worldwide survey taken by the research firm TNS in 2008 (before the explosive rise of social media), the primary activities for which people use the Web include: to consult an information search engine (81 percent); read the

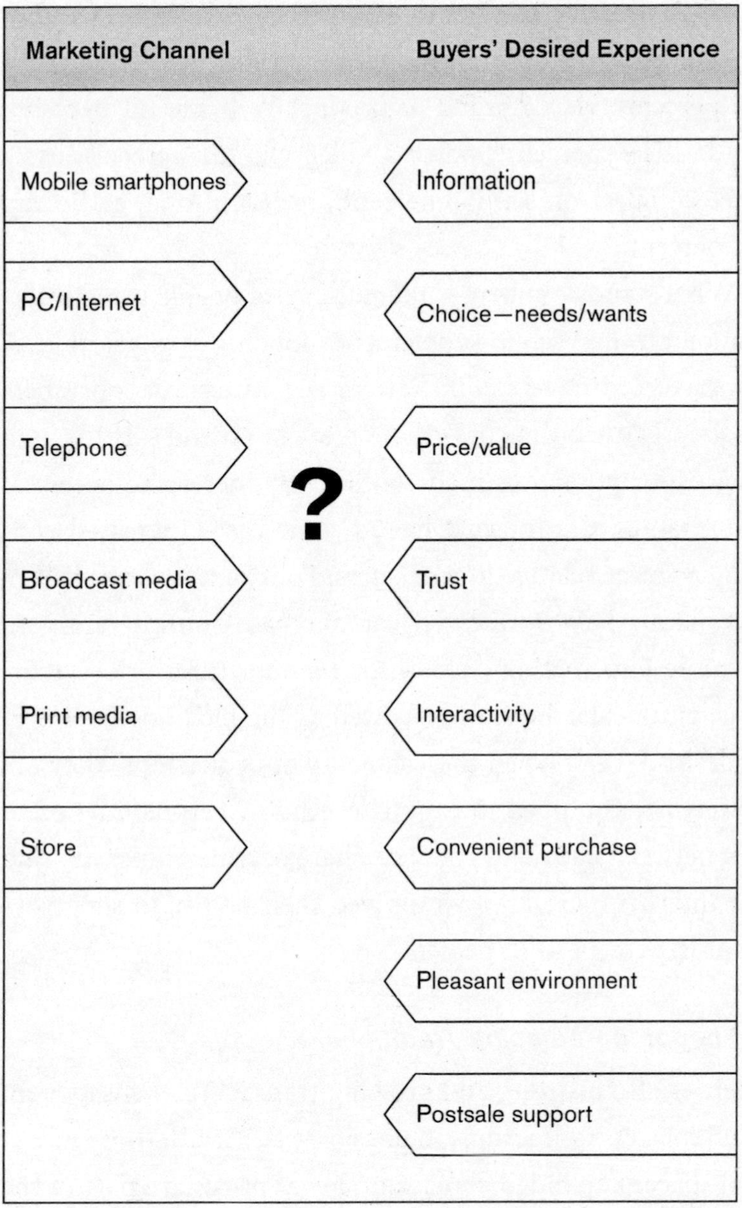

Marketing Channel	Buyers' Desired Experience
Mobile smartphones	Information
PC/Internet	Choice—needs/wants
Telephone	Price/value
Broadcast media	Trust
Print media	Interactivity
Store	Convenient purchase
	Pleasant environment
	Postsale support

?

FIGURE 6. Potential Gaps Between What Marketing Channels Deliver and Customers Desire

news (76 percent); bank online (74 percent); check the weather (65 percent); research a product or service before buying it (63 percent); visit a brand or product Web site (61 percent); pay bills (56 percent); watch a video clip (51 percent); use a price comparison site (50 percent); or listen to an audio clip (44 percent).[4]

What stands out here is the number of people using information on the Web to supplement shopping at physical locations. According to a 2008 Pew survey, American consumers frequently use online information to search and sort through choices for purchases made offline.[5] By increasing access to information, the Internet has in some cases increased consumer power relative to marketers. For example, over half of automobile buyers research car purchases online and gain accurate information concerning manufacturer prices, margins, and dealer incentives as well as the blue book value of trade-ins.[6] Then when they show up at dealerships, they are powerfully equipped to negotiate. Another Pew study found that between 2001 and 2006 the share of Americans who said the Internet had greatly improved their ability to shop rose from 16 percent to 32 percent.[7]

E-Shopping Replacing Traditional Shopping

There is also a strong and growing transactional component that replaces transactions in physical places with those in virtual space. Expanded choice and lower prices are part of the reason people buy online, but convenience is also important. As exemplified by online banking, consumers have flocked to e-commerce sites that allow greater convenience and control—and often lower cost—in exchange for self-service. For instance, today a majority of U.S. leisure and unmanaged business travelers book online.[8] Essentially such businesses displace traditional intermediaries that are now perceived as adding insufficient value.

As is well known, consumers have embraced e-shopping for digitized products such as software, video, and music. In these cases, e-shopping offers convenience and nearly instantaneous delivery as well as the ability to sample a free snippet of media, or a trial version of software. Automated recommendation services and other online information sources take the place of knowledgeable salespeople. And because inventory of digitized goods has negligible costs, it's relatively easy to buy rare or backlist products that would be nearly impossible to track down offline. Correspondingly, consumers have demonstrated a reluctance to pay for something they know costs virtually nothing to deliver; that has kept prices low, or in the extreme case, has led to illegal downloading and file sharing.

In contrast to digitized products, less than 1 percent of consumer packaged goods sales in the United States were made through online channels in 2009.[9] Shopping online for such items requires waiting for delivery, whereas shopping at physical locations offers the gratification of instant possession. Further, once consumers are in a store, scanning store shelves for items is scarcely more time-consuming than browsing through e-retailer pages online. Plus, consumers balk at online shipping charges that are very high relative to an item's cost, and not all online retailers provide greater choice than their physical counterparts.

Consumer packaged goods manufacturers who sell directly to shoppers online risk alienating their retail partners. However, one advantage to managing a proprietary e-tailer site is being able to offer items that offline retailers have removed from their shelves or have no space to stock. For example, Neutrogena offers hundreds of skin-care items online, while grocery stores and drugstores can carry only a fraction of them. Although evidence is mixed on this point, some observers argue that for product categories with "long tails"—that is, those that contain a large proportion of items that are sold infrequently—overall consumer demand for the category will end up increasing, since the availability of more items means offerings are better matched to tastes.[10]

Social Media plus Familiar Places

Without a doubt, the most explosive growth in online services is in the realm of social media. Networking sites have taken off for their ability to create an enveloping, unique user experience that has no real offline equivalent. Just as important, nearly all the content is user-generated, though some comes from advertisers. YouTube has 449 million unique monthly visitors, while Facebook is the most trafficked global site as measured in minutes, with 6 billion plus minutes spent on it per day, by its more than 500 million active users (those who have returned to the site in the last 30 days).[11] In 2009, 804 million people used global networking sites, representing a 19 percent increase from the year before.[12]

Supposedly, the ability to make new friends and connect to people anywhere, regardless of their physical location, is one of the appeals of social media and social networking. However, one study found that half of Facebook friends are in the same metropolitan area; for teenage users, as many as 90 percent of friends are in the same area.[13] Another found that people use Facebook more to solidify existing or geographically near relationships than to initiate or continue geographically distant ones.[14] Echoing the division of America into 9 nations, an analysis of 210 million Facebook profiles divided the country into 7 regions on the basis of links with friends. Within these regions there were strong local clusters and few connections outside them, with one of the exceptions being a New York–Los Angeles tie.[15] That is, electronically enabled social networks remain remarkably local for most users.

Marketers can turn these proximity patterns to advantage. As consumers continue to share retailer preferences, product reviews, and online promotions through social networks, the geographic concentration of friend-to-friend links will make it easier to target customers according to where they live and to coordinate online and offline programs.

Variance in Online Marketing Receptivity

One might expect consumers to have similar views toward online and traditional advertising, or to appreciate Web ads more, if the information is targeted based on online behaviors and is thus more personally relevant. In fact, a 2009 Nielsen survey indicated that Internet users distinguish between online and offline advertising and also make sharp distinctions among different forms of online advertising: 70 percent of consumers have some degree of trust in brand Web sites and 64 percent in brand sponsorships versus the 55 percent to 62 percent having some degree of trust in radio, outdoor, magazine, newspaper, and TV advertising. However, a mere 24 percent of consumers have some level of trust in text ads on mobile phones; 33 percent in online banner ads; 37 percent in online video ads; and 41 percent in search engine result ads.[16] This suggests that both the mode of delivery and the location of ads in virtual space are significant factors in establishing trust.

The fact that Burberry, to take just one example, has more than one million "fans" on Facebook sounds impressive. But, despite the options available, relatively few people engage very actively with marketers in virtual space. A Pew survey of consumers using the Web to research or buy music, cell phones, and housing found that 5 percent or fewer posted online ratings of products after purchase.[17] Still another Pew survey found some evidence of Internet and social network fatigue: 7 percent of Americans use the Internet as their primary means of social communication, yet feel conflicted about all that interconnectivity. Primarily male and in their late twenties, this group also uses electronic devices for entertainment but "many think it is good to take a break from online use."[18] If the fatigue spreads, it would hardly be surprising if marketers and their brands were among the first connections to be dropped.

Marketing in Virtual Space

To succeed, disruptive new products or processes typically have to be better, cheaper, or faster than those they replace. Consumers clearly have welcomed efficiencies in Internet retailing of physical products, delivery of digitized goods, and performance of services that either stand alone or augment offline or online goods. What may be less obvious is the extent to which superior understanding of physical distribution, online-offline coordination, and customer location contribute to marketers' online success.

The Two Types of E-Retailer Genesis

Since the dot-com boom and bust of the late 1990s, e-retailing has achieved steady growth. Amazon, America's number one online retailer, started out as a Web business, as did Newegg (number nine) and Netflix (number eighteen). Both Dell (number two) and L.L.Bean (number twenty-two) came from catalog businesses and QVC (number eleven) originated in television sales. Interestingly, though, the majority of the top fifty online retail businesses are also conventional brick-and-mortar retailers, with Staples and Office Depot at number 2 and number 4, respectively; Apple, whose significant physical retail operations we explored in the last chapter, is at number five.[19] This suggests that efficiencies gained from running both online and offline operations are a competitive advantage. Firms that are in e-retail only save on the costs of running a retail store. But for physical products, they still need warehouses, inventory, and transportation. It also suggests that achieving brand recognition and attracting a loyal customer base on the Internet is difficult. Single-retailer sites are generally less effective in drawing in traffic than are search engine, social networking, or information-aggregator sites.

Amazon is one of the few success stories to emerge from the first e-commerce boom. The site succeeded by providing consumers with choice, price, and convenience; patiently investing huge amounts of cash in warehouses to store an unprecedented assortment of physical products; and achieving shipping efficiencies so as to minimize product delivery times. In another turn of the revolving wheel of retailing that we referred to in the preceding chapter, splitting information search and ordering from physical delivery actually harkens back to the days before self-service when merchants delivered orders to customers. Amazon is the eighth largest retailer in the United States for Pampers, which is awkwardly bulky for consumers to transport home from the store but relatively easy and inexpensive to deliver via mail.

Along with Amazon, a few other pure e-retailers have joined the ranks of the top fifty e-retailers by adopting the category killer format—carrying an in-depth assortment of items in one or more product categories. In these cases, overall demand for the brand or product category may be widespread across geographies but demand for an individual variant within a local trading area may be small. The online retailer Zappos, for example, offers a huge assortment of shoes—branded products with a massive number of stock-keeping units representing different combinations of size, color, and style. Zappos does not necessarily offer the lowest prices to be found on the Web, but it provides high levels of choice and customer service, including free shipping both ways.

Whereas Amazon and Zappos achieved success through centralization, eBay took the opposite approach—acting solely as a broker and payment agent between dispersed buyers and sellers, and removing itself entirely from the physical transfer of goods between the two. Sellers in the giant online marketplaces created by eBay took on these functions. Thanks to the expenses of transnational shipping, the complexities of passing through customs, as well as the fees involved in international currency exchange, transactions in the eBay marketplaces conformed to national (or EU) boundaries.

The point here is that opening an online store does not, in and of itself, create value. Both Amazon and eBay found ways to unlock value tied up in traditional transaction and distribution systems.

E-Retailing and Channel Coordination

When firms have both online and offline operations, marketers must integrate their strategies for virtual and physical place, especially when targeting customer segments who shop both channels. Ford still requires a nationwide network of local dealers where consumers can obtain new cars and get them serviced. But, increasingly, consumers research brands, features, and models on the Internet. So, rather than visiting six or seven dealerships in person, they may only visit two or three. Such consumers expect the online and offline arms of a business to know what the other is doing and to be able to switch back and forth between the two.

One way this plays out is through integrated ordering and inventory management. For example, Best Buy allows customers to place orders online (thus eliminating the need to travel to several stores) for in-store pickup (thus eliminating shipping fees)—at a price savings thanks to the elimination of shipping charges. Before 2009, Nordstrom's Web store drew on its own dedicated inventory and warehouse; and if an item was out of stock there, it lost the sale. Now Nordstrom's Web store offers the entire stock from all 115 regular stores; shoppers can choose to have an item delivered directly to their home or to the nearest store, where they can inspect it before buying. Multichannel same-store sales increased 7 percent the year following the change.[20] Conversely, if an item is out of stock in-store, L.L.Bean helps customers to place an online order while they are still in the store, for at-home delivery later.

Pricing must also be coordinated, although a number of strategies are possible. Consumers may expect lower online prices thanks to lower costs, but such sales could cannibalize offline sales. If the online store is positioned as carrying out-of-season or promotional stock, then lower online prices may not hurt local outlets. Conversely, some firms, like Sony and Levi's, use their online stores as showcases to establish a (high) reference price for other channels.[21] To the extent that the majority of online customers would never shop at a brick-and-mortar store, and vice versa, greater or lesser price differentiation is possible. For example, T-Mobile charged twenty dollars to forty dollars more for handsets sold to mobile phone purchasers who visited a physical store and completed the purchase and activation process there than they did to those who conducted the transaction online.

The Significance of Customer Location Information

One of the virtues of e-retailing is the ability to serve individual consumers no matter where they live. This doesn't mean that geography no longer matters in online retailing. For instance, it is easy for online retailers to serve customers who come to them, but difficult for these stores to identify and target prospective customers. Some online retailers may discover that their best prospects are consumers who live in localities where the retailers' products appeal to only a minority of consumers—meaning that physical stores are less likely to stock these items. An example would be a toy store catering to families with young children who live in a graying suburb. Perhaps less obviously, online retailers should also look out for geographical clusters in their customer base produced by personal, offline word of mouth. That is to say trusted friends tell family and neighbors who share similar needs—and local retail conditions—about their favorite online shopping destinations. A retailer could potentially amplify this word-of-mouth contagion by buying search keywords filtered by zip-code data.[22]

Google has been a particularly potent marketing tool for small businesses with limited geographical reach. Previously, such businesses advertised in increasingly cumbersome yellow pages directories and in the classified sections of local newspapers. Google gave them the opportunity to advertise locally and to appear in paid searches when, for example, a consumer searched for a particular service in a particular town or zip code. Tags highlighting the location of a small business and a special promotion—and costing as little as one dollar per day—can appear on Google Maps. Google intensified its focus on local merchants and local advertising revenue with its 2011 purchase of Zagat local restaurant guide well known for their trusted user-generated content.

Groupon, which has thrived on selling deep-discount offers from local merchants to consumers, represents another type of online service helping small businesses find and attract customers. Consumers who sign up for Groupon receive a daily e-mail offer tailored to where they live and the types of businesses whose offers they have responded to in the past. The promotions are designed to trigger both immediate action and consumer word of mouth: a typical Groupon offer is time limited—expiring within a day—and gives consumers the chance to buy a coupon good for 50 percent or more off a local business's goods or services. A deal activates only when a specified number of consumers purchase the coupon, so consumers are motivated to spread the offer to friends.

E-Commerce and Establishing Trustworthiness

Among the successes from the first generation of Web marketing are services such as e-brokerages for investments;

e-banking for checking and savings; and e-travel services for booking airlines, hotels, and rental cars. Direct-to-consumer digital services reduced or eliminated the need for physical branch locations; cut out costs; improved accuracy or added value through automated information systems; and empowered consumers. Charles Schwab, for example, was an established brand in the brokerage services business when it launched Schwab.com in early 1998. The site provided investors with a suite of analytical tools and timely information to use in making investment decisions for stocks, bonds, and mutual funds. Customers could personalize their home pages and place direct orders—including after-hours trading—all for prices that were lower than competing full-service brokerages. Similarly, investor-owned Vanguard Group, which built its business around low-fee mutual funds, launched Vanguard .com to provide customers greater personalization and round-the-clock information while reducing costs associated with mailings and telephone customer service representatives.

To participate in transactional and even informational online activities, consumers must trust faceless online businesses with sensitive personal information, such as credit-card or bank-account numbers, travel itineraries, reading preferences, or search histories on medical conditions. Many have been willing to do so. Younger generations, especially, are less concerned with security and privacy issues than older generations: some younger users are even posting all their credit-card transactions on a social media site called Blippy.com.

However, consumers' willingness to share personal financial

data rests on their belief that businesses have systems in place that can securely and accurately process the information. This suggests that established offline firms may enjoy an advantage in setting up online operations. In the physical world, small local banks, stock brokers, and insurance agents can compete against national firms, in part because face-to-face customer contact and participation in local social and business networks lower customers' risk perceptions. Strictly online services do not share these qualities and it may be much more difficult for small, unknown challengers in data-dependent categories to compete successfully.

The connection between geographical location and trust is also a factor in online marketplaces. Just as most Facebook friends are in close proximity, so do eBay buyers display a bias toward trading with sellers in the same city or nearby area. The same pattern holds for the Spanish online marketplace MercadoLibre. Presumably, the underlying reason is that the buyer can more easily trace the seller in the event of dissatisfaction or misrepresentation of the product.[23]

Engaging with Consumers

The second generation of the Web is characterized by consumer-created content and social networks—from Twitter and Facebook to YouTube and Myspace—that allow users to interact. Naturally, advertisers hope to insinuate their brands into the conversation, and while this can be difficult, there have been notable successes. Ford's spokesperson in social media, Scott Monty, is one of the company's best-known employees and a contributor to Ford's goal for its virtual presence—to be informative and engaging, without being intrusive—and has helped get the brand onto the consideration list of as many consumers as possible.

In the past couple of years, Adidas found that messages delivered through social media achieved a five times higher return than those delivered through television, attracting over two million fans to a Facebook page. Dell generated sales by using Twitter to alert consumers to promotions. Mountain Dew, whose soft drinks target younger demographics, spent most of its 2009 budget on its year-long "DEWmocracy 2" campaign online. Using Facebook, Twitter, YouTube, and other social media networks and tools, four thousand of the brand's most loyal consumers helped to cocreate three new beverages. In addition to selecting flavors, colors, names, and package design, the fans also collaborated in creating television ads, online media planning and buying, and leading grassroots campaigns in a nationwide contest to select the final winning addition to the product line. In a twelve-week period, the limited-time offering of flavor finalists yielded over seventeen million cases worth approximately one hundred million dollars at retail.[24]

Some contend that such aspects of social media will revolutionize marketing. For several reasons, we are skeptical about how far-reaching any changes will be. First, social media will not alter the main purpose and principles of marketing, which is to acquire and retain a customer by serving his or her needs. Second, though social networks magnify its potential importance, the impact of word-of-mouth recommendations has long been recognized by marketers. Third, Facebook, Twitter, and other social media are not subscription based, and so, they—like print or broadcast media before them—have to rely on paid advertising or marketer sponsorships to cover their costs. Finally, marketers have a long history of leveraging new media as they come onstream while retaining existing media. Television did not kill newspaper advertising. Direct mail boosted rather than cannibalized retail store sales. Rather than revolutionizing marketing, the use of social media can improve it—in areas like market research, new product development, customer interactions, brand positioning, targeting, and content creation.

On the other hand, marketers face twin challenges: They have less control over social media than other online or traditional media, and the reach and frequency of consumer word of mouth is greatly amplified. A particular concern is that consumers trust their peers more than marketers; the Nielsen survey mentioned above found that 90 percent of Internet users trust recommendations from people they know and 70 percent trust strangers' opinions posted online.[25] Good marketers are increasingly aware that any misstep can be transmitted nearly instantaneously around the world, and therefore monitor what is being said about their brands online.

One obvious advantage of social media is that, even more so than direct-mail and telephone marketers, online advertisers can easily collect and store behavioral data about customer response to promotions. Web site owners can track people's movements across Web pages, including which site they came from and which site they went to next. The danger is that the "creepiness factor" for customers escalates as marketers increasingly experiment with following consumers around on their Web travels. For example, a consumer who looked at a pair of shoes on Zappos.com may find that, for weeks afterwards, ads for that particular shoe pop up on unrelated sites she visits.[26] Such practices may threaten to erode consumers' trust in a Web site.

Another potential danger for marketers is that as consumers spend more time online, the chances of a security or privacy breach with huge ramifications may increase. Both Facebook and Google have flirted with potentially disastrous privacy policies,[27] and if such events trigger more stringent privacy regulations—say, blocking use of behavioral data to target online consumers—Web marketers may have to resort to traditional and less specific bases of segmentation, such as the geographical location of a user's Internet provider (IP) address. Web marketers may also choose to advertise on social media platforms based on geographical affinities. For example, Myspace users have tended to be located in smaller cities and communities in the south and central parts of the country.[28] Even though Myspace, which was one of the first wildly popular social media sites, is falling behind Facebook, as of late 2009, it still had 70 million U.S. users who logged on every month (versus 90 million for Facebook and 20 million for Twitter)—and this audience could be a prime demographic for certain advertisers.

Mobile Commerce and the Return
of Place

More than any other electronic device or marketing channel, mobile phones are the most personal medium. They are the one portable media device that nearly all owners have with them everywhere, all the time.[29] They are an extension of the person, an essential part of daily life and routine. Users domesticate them with special ring tones, wallpapers, photos, music, and games—and such downloads are themselves a huge business. Moreover, mobiles have proven to be extraordinarily adaptable devices for enabling marketing exchanges. In Japan, they are used like debit cards to make payments. In developing countries, their use as payment systems will be increasingly important, particularly in rural areas. The convergence of music, live TV streaming, and games—such as on the iPhone—is very attractive to consumers, especially in developing countries, where the lower costs of buying one mobile phone rather than multiple devices are especially pertinent.[30]

Adoption of mobile devices far exceeds desktop Internet adoption. Globally, there were some 4 billion mobile users in 2008, nearly 3 times the number of Internet users.[31] The spread is especially large in emerging economies, where the majority of mobile phones are standard—that is, unconnected to, or with limited connections to, the Internet. But smartphones with Web browsers, keyboards, and video capability that operate on 3G or 4G networks or Wi-Fi are rapidly gaining market share. In

Japan and South Korea, where 3G was launched as early as 2001, penetration exceeds 70 percent. In the United States and Western Europe, smartphones captured more than 30 percent of the mobile market following the introduction of the iPhone in 2007; by the end of 2010, globally there may be over a billion 3G subscribers.[32] In the United States alone, the mobile Web approached 100 million unique users per month in 2010.

The key to this growth is the quality of the user experience. Mobile Web browsers may be limited in terms of screen size, page-loading speed, and compatible software compared to personal computer (PC) browsers, but these disadvantages pale in the face of on-the-go access, the combination of telephone plus data, and good-quality images. A 2009 Pew survey reported that close to a third of American adults used mobile devices to surf the Web—up from a fourth in 2007. The PC's capacity for storing personal settings and files becomes less of a comparative advantage when mobile users can store files in the "cloud" of databases reachable by easy-to-use phone apps. It turns out that smartphones are largely being used for data transmission and media consumption, as opposed to voice calls. Networks are having difficulty keeping up with surging demand from heavy data users, whose numbers are likely to exceed 1 billion in 2013.[33]

Many standard mobile phones carry an embedded GPS chip that allows network operators to pinpoint the phone's location. Smartphones allow consumers to see and share location information. Through special apps, including "Places" for Facebook, it's possible to merge your coordinates with online maps, send your current location to friends, and receive information about your surroundings. Firms such as Twitter, Facebook, Yelp, Foursquare, Loopt, Groupon, Gowalla, and Google are joining in the battle for geolocation supremacy.

Letting location-based mobile apps know where they are allows consumers to search for information relevant to their immediate surroundings. Transportation applications—the time interval until the next train or bus, or the location of a Zipcar—improve the commuting experience. Or consumers can ask for the times of movie showings within, say, a ten-block radius. In searching for product information, they can take a picture of an item's bar code and receive comparative price information for nearby retailers. According to Deloitte & Touche, consumers expect to use mobile apps to find store locations (55 percent); research prices (45 percent); find product information (40 percent); find discounts and coupons (32 percent); and make purchases (25 percent).[34]

In some cases, consumers can contribute data about local conditions to online information sources. For example, birders can overlay sightings onto maps. Diners can take photos of a restaurant exterior, interior, or menu and upload these to Yelp. Based on geotag data, the imagery is merged with online maps and reviews of the restaurant. Such reviews increasingly make or break the success of restaurants, hotels, and other service businesses. This new wave of applications that incorporate location technology is changing online advertising, consumer information search, and shopping. See Figure 7 to see how the marketer-driven and consumer-driven elements relate to one another.

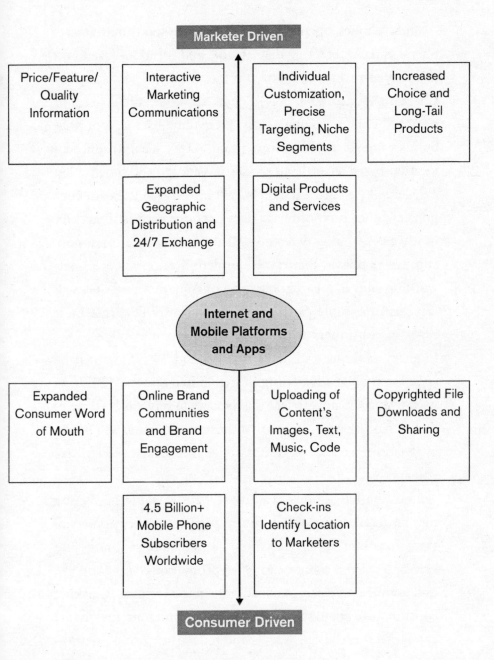

FIGURE 7. Impacts of Internet and Mobile Marketing

Smartphones open up possibilities for sponsored smart-phone apps, interactive display ads, and location-based and augmented-reality ads. For instance, toilet-paper company Charmin sponsored a "SitOrSquat" app that guides users to nearby public restrooms—an incredibly useful tool that builds value for the Charmin brand. AT&T has introduced a location-based advertising service in Chicago and other cities: Triggered by a "geofence," it allows advertisers to beam coupons or other promotional offers to consumers as they enter or leave the vicinity of a store. Meanwhile, as more and more consumers upload their location identification to social networking sites like Facebook and Foursquare, these sites will represent desirable platforms for advertisers to target messages to consumers while they're in particular places. One industry observer estimates that around $3 billion will be spent on mobile advertising in the United States by 2013. As with television, advertisers will be able to buy ads by time of day and location[35]— except that the target location will not be as general as a city zip code but, rather, the precise place where you are.

Location-based apps promise to be a versatile marketing tool for retailers. As well as informing potential customers of store locations, operating hours, merchandise lines, and prices, local merchants can offer promotions and coupons, tied to time and place, to consumers in the vicinity. By asking consumers to opt in to mobile ads and promotions, merchants can target their best prospects and reduce intrusions on unreceptive consumers. In 2010, McDonald's tested a promotion on Foursquare in which consumers who "checked in" to certain McDonald's restaurants could win $5 or $10 gift cards. Participating restaurants saw a 33 percent increase in foot traffic and free publicity in local news media. Using services like Shopkick, marketers can deliver retailer-specific promotional offers to consumers who download a free app. Promotions can also be delivered to consumers whose mobile phone GPS indicates that they are close by a particular store. Participating retailers include Best Buy, Macy's, and Sports Authority.

Mobiles can also serve as loyalty cards. Consumers who check in at a merchant's location via Foursquare, Gowalla, or Loopt can collect loyalty points, which are stored on their mobile phones. After collecting a certain number of points, they can earn a badge that gives them a discount or free item. Starbucks, for example, will give holders of a Foursquare "mayor" badge one dollar off a Frappuccino.

Nevertheless, how well local marketing on mobiles will work hinges on some open questions. Currently, the enabling conditions are not quite in place. First, sending too many unsolicited ads to a mobile will deplete the battery charge and annoy consumers. Second, the security of mobile payment systems must be ironclad. Third, the interfaces of different mobile platforms vary, such that a single advertisement cannot be delivered to all mobile phones. Fourth, cookies are not easily applied to mobile phones for addressability purposes, so marketers would have to tap into the clickstreams of data sent between phones and carriers. If behavioral data is being used as the basis for sending ad messages, European legislators for sure will require an "opt in" by each targeted consumer. In 2010, the European Union started legal proceedings against the British government for allowing the company Phorm to sell clickstream data to Internet service providers for behaviorally targeted advertising purposes.

These technical limitations will no doubt be overcome, but equally important, the mobile phone is a very personal device. Traditionally, carriers didn't allow ads, in part because of concerns about the user experience (who wants a voice mail or e-mail in-box filled up with ads?); in the United States, the fact that users pay for incoming calls means solicitations in this manner will be seen as a nuisance—not good for a company's image. Mobile advertising also involves two kinds of privacy risk: intrusiveness (being contacted against your will) and how sensitive personal data are handled. Marketers will have to ask permission to communicate if they want to be effective. For example, consumers who have already searched an app related to a particular retailer would likely be more receptive. Moreover, a consumer's proximity to a merchant, as signaled by a GPS tracker in a mobile phone, hardly means receptivity.

The data on mobile users' receptivity to advertising is mixed though generally positive. A JiWire survey of mobile users found that slightly over half said they had acted on an advertisement in an app, and nearly one in five said they had directly purchased from an ad in an app in the last month. Over half were willing to share their location to receive more relevant advertising, and three-quarters said they would prefer to download a free, advertising-supported app over paying an up-front fee for the same app.[36] A subsequent JiWire survey confirmed that over half of mobile North American Wi-Fi users—particularly males and people under age fifty-five—were willing to share their locations to receive relevant messages.[37] However, as recently as 2008, in a survey of a more general audience—primary household shoppers in 8 countries—only 18 percent rated mobile advertising based on location as very appealing, although 76 percent thought it would be widespread by 2015.[38]

Assuming that mobile advertising will only expand, marketers need to figure out how to best use it. Consumers on the go may prefer fast and simple messages to slower and more complex information, but the junk e-mail syndrome should be avoided. How many ads do consumers want to see and how many times do they want to see the same ad? Search ads should work well because they are user initiated and concise, with deeper information just one click away. It's likely that much of the mobile traffic—and therefore advertising—will be driven by social networking sites, but what if they prove to be a fad that fades or that only appeals to a few demographic groups? Foursquare-type services may prove even more of a fad. In addition, hyperlocal geotargeting of consumers may draw the net too closely: currently only a small fraction of consumers check in to locations, and this behavior may never spread widely to the mainstream. Even if it does, advertisers will always need to reach beyond the small group of people who are in a specific establishment at a specific time in order to target a larger group of customers within the general geographic area.

The Architecture of Virtual Space

The locations and structures of spaces and places shape people's actions in the virtual world just as much as in the physical world. Some locations beckon, others are impossible to find. Some sites invite a revisit, others an escape. Consumers want to navigate easily from site to site and within sites. Relevant information should be easy to locate and at most one or two clicks away. It's frustrating and irritating to be deadended in the maze of an online menu that leads mostly to irrelevant information or doesn't permit shortcuts. As in the physical world, consumers rely on explicit maps as well as unconscious cues to guide them to their desired destinations.

Although the principles of good architecture in virtual space are well known, they're worth reiterating. Even now, the consumer friendliness of commercial sites can get overlooked in the latest redesign and rush to use the newest technologies. Basic functionality particularly matters for on-the-go users who require simple, intuitive interactivity, won't tolerate pop-ups on small screens, and don't want to hunt through search results or dig down more than a click or two to find the information they're looking for.

Just as in the physical world, online retail siting needs to capitalize on the surrounding infrastructure and ecosystem. In the virtual world, siting is one part acquiring the location and nine parts constructing signposts and links to the location. The first step is securing a good domain name. Marketers who already operate offline will typically want a matching domain name—such as BarnesandNoble.com—or a name that is reasonably close—such as nytimes.com. Purely online marketers have a more expansive range of choices. In the Wild West days of the Internet, entrepreneurs bought up descriptive domain names that could aid in establishing category leadership—such as flowers.com—later selling them to the highest bidder. On the whole, though, less explicit, more creative domain names have succeeded as powerful brands: Yahoo!, Google, and Trulia come to mind. In 2011, the Internet Corporation for Assigned Names and Numbers (ICANN) decided to expand the pool of domain extensions, thus increasing the number of possible domain names. Now, instead of fighting over coveted dot-coms, companies can create their own personal extension—a .ford or .microsoft—thus providing more control over their brand.

The single most important element in virtual location is a site's position on the pages of major search engines. There is no real equivalent in the physical world to the gatekeeping role of Google, Baidu, Bing, or other search engines. It is through their maps of the Internet, constructed on sophisticated algorithms linking user queries with relevant search results, that people find sites; and if potential visitors can't find your site through them, they'll probably never find you. Achieving top placement in paid and unpaid search results is one of the key disciplines in Web architecture and an expertise worth obtaining if you don't already have it.

Second to information search results is placing links on other high-traffic Web pages. The same concept applies as in physical siting—you want to have a presence in high-traffic places. The strategy is analogous to locating a store in a shopping center anchored by a big-name retailer. Putting "pay-per-click" ads on selected smaller sites that appeal to your target customers can also drive significant traffic. Of course, in the virtual world you don't have to relocate your entire store and inventory to find better neighbors; you merely have to create different links.

The act of moving through the virtual spaces and places of the Internet was transformed nearly overnight when the Web replaced text-only content and lists with text-and-image two-dimensional spaces. Thereafter, screen space could be organized into distinct pages with top and bottom, and left, right, and center orientations. Very quickly, the architecture of Web sites adopted common conventions, such as the home page and row of tabs linking to major sections of the site. Most retail sites adopted a similar structure, as did most professional service sites, university sites, and newspaper sites. Almost instinctively, users knew that in a retail site, they could either enter a search term for a specific item or browse through product categories; and they quickly understood they could store items in a shopping cart for eventual purchase or abandonment. These conventions provided the same sense of security as knowing what to expect when entering a hotel, office building, or home. For site owners, the use of standard architectures and navigational features, far from being constraining, frees designers to focus on creating the unique content and the special look and feel of each site.

As with physical places, owners and designers of sites need to think about flow and the length of time consumers spend on various pages. Google, for example, must balance the ad revenue gained from exposing consumers to more advertising with the consumer desire for expedient search.[39] Many newspaper-owned sites give visitors free news content in exchange for pages filled with ads, but if an excess of ads slows down or interferes with loading pages, people will leave. Up to a point, the more time visitors spend on a Web page is an indication of greater interest in the content; beyond that, it may be an indicator of confusion or a sign that the consumer has left that page open but is no longer viewing it.

As the Web has aged, too much complexity unaccompanied by improvements in functionality or customer experience has crept into too many sites. For example, on travel sites, Forrester Research has found signs of poor functionality; inefficient content (such as a lack of visual content describing hotels or destinations); and absence of interactive customer support—"Instead of getting easier, planning and booking travel online has become more complex and confusing during the past decade."[40] It's not a case of untutored users. Travel bookers who encounter problems are no more likely to be older, technophobic, or infrequent travelers than those not encountering problems. Simple displays and interfaces can be the most effective, as witness the enthusiastic reception of the bookstore built into Apple's iPad simply because it displays books in the familiar physical form of a bookshelf.

Thanks to the increase in mobile Web traffic, ease in

navigating sites is becoming an ever more important consideration. Web site designers now must take new factors into consideration: The screen real estate on mobiles is smaller; connection speeds are often slower; and some browsers are unable to run all the software commonly employed to jazz up sites. Site owners need to know exactly what information their users really need rather than giving them everything that's on the regular site. The architecture of mobile sites needs to be clean, simple, and viewable across different mobile browsers. Many older computers and browsers have difficulty handling the latest site designs. Good design will increasingly mean creating formats that work on smartphones, tablets and PCs, dial-up and broadband, and new and legacy browsers.

Few consumers build, design, or commission their own houses. But in virtual space, nearly everyone can acquire the tools and a location for constructing a unique personal space to upload content and connect to others. Sites that nurture these activities have demonstrated huge potential. That's part of the draw of Facebook, which also offers the perceived safety of being a members-only preserve—even if the number of members is in the hundreds of millions. Fashion-oriented social-network sites—such as StyleHive or FashMatch—enable members to upload pictures of fashion looks they've created, assemble virtual outfits from an online inventory of clothes and accessories, share opinions on trends, and click on links to buy favorite brands.

Interestingly, one of the things people like to do in virtual space is to create facsimiles of physical geographies. Second

Life is a popular 3-D virtual world where consumers can rent or buy land, build and furnish houses, populate them with avatars, travel through the world, and exchange real money. SimFarm and other farming games offer rural alternatives to the urban life of SimCity. In 2010, FarmVille was the number one game played on Facebook, and FrontierVille was number three. Players can invite friends to homestead next door, help each other out, and join cooperatives. In other words, consumers express their longing for community and special places in the virtual world just as much as they do in the physical world.

Geographical Variations in the Enablers for Virtual Space

It's sometimes easy to forget that the virtual world is dependent on places in the physical world (see Figure 8). Most critically, without the networks of cables or fiber optics, or the proper spacing of wireless towers and satellite transmitters, no one would have access. The physical infrastructure must keep pace with changing demand, and the fact that demand is not spread evenly among users must also be considered. In the United States, AT&T agreed to sell a flat-rate plan with the iPhone but seriously underestimated the burden that the surging demand from heavy data users would place on the physical network, especially in technophile cities like New York and San Francisco.

E-Commerce Elements	Physical Locations
Infrastructure	ISP and mobile network infrastructures serving targeted geographical areas Corporate data servers located onsite or offsite
Products	Manufacturing and warehousing of physical goods sold via e-commerce
Advertising	Offline media, such as newspapers, magazines, billboards
Purchase Transactions	Bricks and mortar outlet affiliated with e-commerce site
Product Delivery	Physical goods delivered from centralized warehouses or geographically dispersed seller locations
Consumption	Physical goods consumed at home, work, etc. Digital information converted to physical form, e.g., airline tickets, CDs, etc. Digital goods consumed on either stationary electronic devices located at home or workplace or on mobile device

FIGURE 8. Examples of Physical Locations Involved in E-Commerce

Currently Internet penetration is highest in North America, Western Europe, and the industrialized parts of Asia Pacific, but geographical coverage is changing. Growth rates in the rest of Asia, Africa, and South America are expected to exceed growth in the more mature markets; by 2013 the five countries with the largest number of Internet users will include China, the United States, India, Japan, and Brazil.[41] It is predicted that by 2013 the total number of Internet users will reach 2.2 billion, or about 30 percent of the projected global population of 7 billion[42]—up from about a quarter of the world's population who were Internet users in 2009.[43]

Internet usage has been abetted by the growing availability of access points, including access from work, home, cybercafes, schools, libraries, and airports. Increasingly, access is being driven by mobile phones with 3G, 4G, or Wi-Fi capabilities, and it is estimated that by 2013, the installed base of phones with Internet access will surpass the installed base of personal computers.[44] In developing markets, access to virtual space will depend on meeting affordability criteria for the physical devices needed to connect to telecommunications networks—in the range of a hundred-dollar computer or a twenty-dollar unsubsidized mobile handset.[45]

For e-marketers other types of enablers also vary across geographies. For example, e-retailing that sells physical products over the Internet requires both payment systems and distribution channels to move physical goods. As witness to the importance of payment systems, note that eBay's financial performance is now largely driven by the success of its secure payment system, PayPal. CEO John Donahoe expects revenue from its payment systems to exceed revenue from its marketplace segment in the next few years.[46] In much of Africa, both distribution systems and payment infrastructures are inadequate. In Kenya, though, M-PESA is an innovative service that allows unbanked consumers to transfer money over mobile phones by sending a text message. Over half of the adults in Kenya now use M-PESA to pay for goods and services or to send money to relatives. Physical place still enters in: to load money onto a phone or to receive payment in cash, users must visit an M-PESA outlet, usually located in a shop or gas station.

Another type of infrastructure that varies from place to place is government laws, regulations, and tax policies. A key factor in the growth of U.S. e-retailing has been the inability of state and local governments to levy taxes on goods purchased from online retailers that have no physical presence in their jurisdiction. On many types of consumer purchases, forgone taxes offset delivery charges; this, along with other efficiencies, allows e-retailers to undercut prices of local retailers. At least one economic analysis demonstrated that there is a strong relationship between e-retail sales in a given state and sales tax rates that apply to purchases from offline retailers, which suggests that tax avoidance may be an important contributor to e-retail activity.[47] However, states are now pressuring the federal government to allow collection of taxes in a consumer's home state, which would serve to help level the playing field.

The privacy policies of countries directly impact the ability of Web marketers to identify and track consumers as they use the Web. Officials in South Korea, Italy, Spain, Germany, and

Australia are also investigating Google's privacy practices involving the personal data it collected in the course of introducing its Street View mapping service in those countries.[48] In general, European Union privacy policies place more limits on the collection, use, and storage of personal data gathered by online marketers than do those of the United States.

Google's difficulties in China, noted in the introduction, illustrate the power governments have over companies doing business in virtual space. As the events surrounding 2011's Arab Spring in the Middle East—not to mention uprisings and political protests elsewhere—have illustrated, electronic communications services and online publishers perceived as aiding dissidents are particularly vulnerable to government clampdowns.

In sum, there is no escaping physical space even in the virtual world. From the physical network infrastructure that underpins Internet and wireless communications to the territorial jurisdictions that govern commerce; from the architecture that allows consumers to navigate Web sites, to the linkages between virtual communications and brick-and-mortar commerce, the virtual and the physical are intertwined. In a virtual landscape, marketers would do well to remember that customers still want the same things they always wanted in a retailer—trust, convenience of access, information, and interaction—but this need not be seen as a limitation. As the potential of mobile advertising demonstrates, place-aware innovations around virtual space can create new markets and new ways for marketers and consumers to engage.

Chapter 4

MARKETING GEOGRAPHIC PLACE

The headline of a front-section ad in the January–February 2010 *Harvard Business Review* read "There's only one Lexus plant outside Japan." The advertiser was not Lexus or its parent company Toyota, but the province of Ontario, Canada. Included in the same issue were ads touting "business friendly Bahrain"; "Clean energy. Green technology + Fresh thinking—why businesses are putting down roots in Ireland"; the "best private bank in North America"—Northern Trust; "Do not miss the IAA World Congress in Moscow"; and an understated ad for the Mandarin Oriental hotel group, where a list of world cities comprises the bulk of the text.[1]

So far, we've explained how brands may appeal to consumers by associating themselves with evocative places, as exemplified in the Mandarin Oriental or the International Advertising Association (IAA) ads, or by emphasizing their geographic roots, as in the Northern Trust ad. But the other ads listed are examples of marketing the place as the product. As the Ontario ad demonstrates, places and products or brands can become interlinked. For example, the New York Times reported that a whole genre of Bollywood films uses Switzerland as a backdrop "to convey an ideal of sunshine, happiness, and tranquility."[2] In turn, Switzerland is attracting droves of Indian tourists enchanted with the Swiss locales used in the popular films. The idealized Switzerland of the Bollywood products lends the real Switzerland a set of associations that are creating marketing opportunities in India for Swiss tourism. Catering to this new market segment, tourism officials and hotel managers have seen a doubling of nights booked by Indian tour groups.

Although marketing of places is commonly associated with tourism promotion, it does not stop there. In addition to promoting tourist attractions, countries and cities are competing for foreign direct investment, globally mobile talent, and export markets. In recent decades, Ireland marketed itself as a desirable location for high-tech companies based on its openness to foreign investment, favorable tax policies, entrepreneurial spirit, and highly educated workforce. By 2010, multinational corporations, including pharmaceutical companies like Pfizer and technology firms like Microsoft and Google, accounted for more than a quarter-million jobs and over 70 percent of the country's exports.[3] While a concurrent housing and financing bubble led Ireland to become a financial basket case, requiring an EU bailout, foreign direct investors represented a growth sector of the economy.

Corporations are not the only investors of interest. Places also compete for university students, professionals in science and engineering, or retirees; for example, Texas, Georgia, and the Carolinas draw retirees away from Florida by offering tax incentives and advertising in places like *Southern Living* magazine.[4] Chile promotes its economic, political, and social achievements in part to improve the competitiveness of its exports (researchers find that products from developed countries tend to be viewed more favorably than those from less developed countries[5]). In other words, places are not simply accessories to marketing or part of the external environment. Many places are also the client for marketing or the primary thing being marketed.

The marketing of places taps deeply into psychology since place marketing is as much, or more, about understanding and shaping, reinforcing or changing psychological connotations and associations as it is about featuring geographical or other characteristics. In the case of nation-states, a change-making leader such as President Barack Obama can shape a nation's image and thereby impact the national balance sheet. To take a smaller country, Prime Minister Mahathir Mohamad's leadership in transforming the economy and opening it up to foreign trade and investment enabled Malaysia—a country of only twenty-three million—to aggressively attract multinationals and punch above its weight on the world stage while he was in office. Hosting—more successfully than expected—the

2010 Fédération Internationale de Football Association (FIFA) World Cup soccer games boosted South Africa's global standing. Meanwhile, India took a hit for its shambolic execution of the 2010 Commonwealth Games.

The remainder of this chapter further explores these aspects of place marketing, which is naturally relevant to officials promoting foreign investment and tourism, but also highly relevant to businesses whose corporate reputation or product brands are closely associated with a particular place. All such businesses have a vested interest in promoting a positive place image.

Why Place Marketing Is Important

A successful place marketing campaign can have a direct impact on local economies. In the United States, for example, international visitors spend on average forty-five hundred dollars per person per trip; additional visitors and revenue produce significant bump-on effects on jobs, tax revenues, and the federal budget deficit. Travel and tourism directly affect hotel, transportation, and arts and entertainment enterprises. However, until recently, the United States, in contrast to most other industrialized nations, and many lesser developed countries as well, never had a travel promotion board to market itself to the rest of the world. Tourism marketing was left up to individual states and cities. Only in the face of a worrisome dip in overseas visitors to the United States from 2000 to 2006 and another sharp decline in 2009—altogether representing lost revenues estimated at about $509 billion—did Congress (with bipartisan support) pass legislation aimed at increasing the number of tourists from abroad. Specifically, the 2010 Travel Promotion Act created a public-private corporation charged with developing a centrally coordinated global advertising and communications campaign. Among other things, this corporation was intended to work closely with the Departments of Commerce, Homeland Security, and State to explain U.S. travel security policies.[6] This last provision went to the heart of the problem: Ever since 9/11, the United States had enacted strict travel policies that made it seem unwelcoming to the world; a clampdown on visas restricted who could enter; and tighter security subjected visitors to sometimes humiliating procedures. Advocates of the marketing program estimated it could generate as many as 1.6 million new inbound visitors a year following the release of program funding toward the end of 2011.

The financial benefits of place marketing are not limited to tourism dollars. Places also compete with each other as sites for retailing, offices, and manufacturing plants and as desirable residential communities. In virtually every locality, building construction and associated services—including real estate and insurance agencies, banking and legal services—are a vital element of the economy.

In his book *Who's Your City?*, Richard Florida points out that "For the first time ever, a huge number of us have the freedom and economic means to choose our place. That means we have an incredible opportunity to find the place that fits us best."[7]

Where you work and live affects your career and finances, closeness to family and friends, and proximity to the social, cultural, or environmental opportunities that make you happy. Whether the right place is an urban area, a smaller city, or the countryside, there is an enormous array of choices. There are marked differences from rust belt to Sunbelt, from older suburb to new planned community, or between the two coastal, technology hubs of San Francisco and Boston. For places seeking to attract well-off retirees, competitive rankings on quality of life published by organizations such as the American Association of Retired Persons (AARP) are an important determinant.

Business executives make equivalent decisions on places to locate offices and plants, looking at factors such as technological expertise, workforce skills availability, tax incentives, and proximity to transportation and to raw materials to distinguish one place from another. When seeking to expand operations or investments overseas, executives weigh all these elements plus political stability, sound fiscal and monetary policies, binding property rights and legal contracts, absence of corruption, and perhaps language skills and culture. Many of these factors enter into the World Bank rankings of country competitiveness. *Newsweek*'s 2010 ranking of the best countries in the world considered five categories of national well-being—education, health, quality of life, economic competitiveness, and political environment.[8]

The result of these high stakes is that places are jostling for our attention and our business. With 193 members of the United Nations, the international stage resembles the cluttered breakfast cereal aisle of a supermarket. Countries and cities are competing with each other in the global economy for foreign investors, consumers of their exports, visitors, and highly skilled workers. Nation-states are also competing in the political realm for influence, strong alliances, and key appointments to lead international organizations. Wealthier and historically powerful places have an advantage out of the starting gate, but increasingly positive images of countries such as South Korea, Peru, and Ghana have helped to secure leadership roles in the United Nations and regional political and economic organizations.

Place identity also matters internally. Thanks to expansion of global business operations and cross-country migration, places are increasingly confronted with tensions between local values and ways of life and the changes resulting from these trends. Western European nations and cities, for example, have struggled to assimilate floods of immigrants from Turkey, North Africa, and Eastern Europe. Eastern European countries that joined the European Union have struggled to retain talented young workers since cross-border barriers separating them from higher paying jobs have been removed. In the last three decades, economic reforms in China opened the country to a huge influx of foreign direct investment, wide exposure to Western consumerism, and, some worry, an erosion of traditional Chinese culture. Thus, a place identity that promotes local pride and cohesion but also builds the confidence to embrace change is a valuable asset for any community or country. It also creates a virtuous loop wherein a good place image boosts confidence and therefore economic and social performance, which in turn further boosts the place image (see Figure 9).

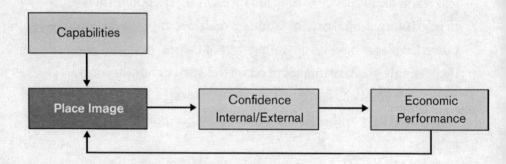

FIGURE 9. Place Image and Performance

How Places Can Market Themselves

Places are the sum of many parts, including such indelible elements as history and physical location, and to talk of reducing a place to a brand or image or single positioning may therefore seem glib. However, the vast majority of outsiders may have no knowledge of a place, or if they do it may be inaccurate or hazy at best. As in product marketing, place marketing seeks to favorably position, or reposition, an object in people's mental maps. Marketing programs can range from sophisticated global campaigns designed to promote nations as destinations for direct foreign investment down to smaller campaigns that seek to put individual towns on the map as tourist destinations. Such differentiating claims may be based on historical events, natural wonders, or productive assets. Gilroy, California, for example, proclaims itself to be the garlic capital of the United States and hosts an annual garlic festival that averages more than a hundred thousand visitors each year.

Positioning

When marketing a city, nation, or other place it's necessary to develop a positioning strategy that sets forth the distinctive strengths and benefits of the place that will connect it with memorable and positive associations in people's mental maps. If a place does not position itself, it is at the mercy of the unpredictable news cycle. The basic steps involved in developing a clear positioning are to identify the audiences the place wishes to address (such as tourists, overseas consumers, and foreign direct investors); assess the perceptions these audiences currently hold; develop a superiority claim about what the place offers that others don't; and articulate the reasons why the superiority claim should be believed.

It may be painful for anyone marketing a city or country to discover that only 1 percent of the world's population knows that it even exists, but it is important to measure awareness and to understand perceptions—both favorable and unfavorable—held by key target audiences both at home and abroad. In order to know what corrective or supplemental messages to present, it is essential to analyze the gaps between perception and reality (both current and intended), for each target group.

What sorts of claims are possible or advisable? First off, a place's positioning and image must be congruent with readily observable reality. In the age of the Internet, twenty-four-hour-a-day news, and easy travel, no place can control or suppress information that shapes its image. For example, it would be unwise for Maine to position itself as a place of warm, friendly people in the way that Hawaii features the Aloha spirit. Second, the claims should support an inclusive vision, relevant to both citizens and potential outside customers in the target audience. Maine's citizens can take pride in the state's pristine, rugged beauty and outdoor recreational activities that have attracted generations of summer visitors from the rest of New England and elsewhere. Third, the claims should incorporate unique, special qualities of the place that keep it from being easily imitated by or confused with other places. These qualities may be the place's culture and history, famous inhabitants, cultural achievements, special physical setting, prominence in world affairs, or well-known companies and products (see Figure 10). For example, many think of Finland as the home of Laplanders and reindeer, Finlandia vodka and Nokia phones.

A potent superiority claim is the presence of industry clusters, which leading business strategist Michael Porter defines as "geographic concentrations of interconnected companies, specialized suppliers, service providers, and associated institutions in a particular field ... that arise because they increase

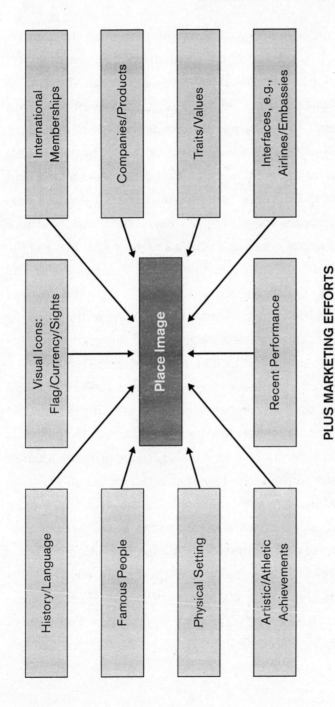

FIGURE 10. Aspects of Place Image

the productivity with which companies can compete."[9] Silicon Valley and North Carolina's research triangle, for instance, both developed reputations as centers of scientific innovation and excellence. Within Silicon Valley, the city of Mountain View is home to a cluster of entrepreneurial companies in the business of social networking that are attracted by the proximity to state-of-the-art thinking and technology incubators. In this age of globalization, when open markets, advanced telecommunications, and cheap transportation allow companies to operate nearly anyplace, Porter's data show that many of the traditional roles of colocation in fostering the development and interchange of specialized knowledge and skills remain extremely advantageous. Furthermore, owing to the complexity of interlocking capabilities upon which clusters depend, this source of advantage is difficult for other places to replicate.

In particular, a unique and supportable superiority claim helps places to avoid competing on price. Offering nothing but tax credits and discounts to attract new factories and jobs ends up being counterproductive. It is also not the primary criterion that serious corporations use in selecting places in which to invest.[10] And the money—or people—attracted by price competition is apt to leave one place as soon as another one promotes a better deal. Countries like Vietnam and Cambodia, for example, picked up some apparel production contracts formerly located in China as Chinese wages rose. Likewise, companies may find ways to take advantage of price deals without benefiting the place offering them. New Zealand learned this the hard way. Before 2005, its immigration policy contained a special category for people applying for residence who invested one million New Zealand dollars in the country. Taking advantage of a loophole, investors put their money in holding companies that didn't actually invest locally.[11]

As a rule of thumb, a clear positioning can be stated in twenty words or less. A number of cities and countries market themselves as trade gateways. Singapore, for example, traditionally positioned itself as the best entry point to Asia for Western multinationals—a position backed up by laws, institutions, and an educated English-speaking work force that made doing business from there safe and easy. For similar reasons, Shanghai has historically been the international commercial center of China. The Netherlands sells itself as a logistics gateway to Europe, claiming that 78 percent of Europe's population can be reached by road and rail within 24 hours. Other types of positionings include Switzerland's as a neutral safe haven for confidential financial services, which is historically well grounded in government and private-sector actions to defend numbered bank accounts. Meanwhile, leveraging its history of democracy and rejection of a standing army, Costa Rica has positioned itself as a peaceful haven for ecotourism and American retirees.

Repositioning

Of course, memorable associations can sometimes stand in the way of new positioning, and it is often harder to unfreeze an existing, perhaps outdated, image in order to build a new one than to start with a clean slate. Consider two examples: The first—a success—is Spain, which in the late 1980s emerged from the regime of Francisco Franco as a vibrant burgeoning democracy within the European Union. To update its outmoded image as a closed, dictatorial society, Spain's business and political leaders worked together to restore national pride and economic performance. The artist Joan Miro's sun image was selected as a visual symbol for the country and is still used in tourism promotion today. In 1986, Barcelona won the competition to host the 1992 Olympics over rival cities Amsterdam, Brisbane, Birmingham, and Paris—in part by emphasizing both modern and historical strengths—a newly cohesive Spain, transcending differences with the Catalonia region of which Barcelona was the capital, and the five hundredth anniversary of the discovery of America by Christopher Columbus. The financial and popular success of the Barcelona Olympics showcased the new Spain to the world. Economic performance was aided by the European Union's implementation of the single-market program to reduce non-tariff barriers and boost intra-European trade. Meanwhile, Spain backed up its new image with public sector reforms and improved infrastructure; Spanish gross domestic product (GDP) accelerated throughout the 1990s.

The second—less successful—example is that of the "Cool Britannia" marketing program (as it was dubbed by the press), launched in the late 1990s under Prime Minister Tony Blair in an effort to update perceptions of Britain. Seeking to promote the emergence of a new knowledge economy to investors and tourists, Britain's policymakers wanted to teach the world about British creativity, adventurousness, and entrepreneurship in science, technology, and business. But where the designers of the Spanish marketing effort needed to start with a clear break from the past, Britain—"this royal throne of kings, this scepter'd isle . . . this precious stone set in the silver sea," as lauded by Shakespeare in *Richard II*—was widely known and admired for things traditional (the monarchy, the museums, and Merchant Ivory movies), all of which brought in substantial tourism dollars each year. Importantly, there was a disconnect between the "Cool Britannia" positioning and the values of the British people. Although a number of task forces devised communications strategies, the campaign never really got off the ground and the whole idea of it was widely derided in the media, particularly outside London. Cynical media commentators and ordinary citizens also poked fun at the very idea of "rebranding" a country like a packaged consumer product. Any expectations that the campaign would produce quick results were dispelled by a survey published by the British Council two years into the effort. Not surprisingly, the research showed that people in other countries continued to see Britain as highly traditional (but favorably so). The campaign lasted around three years before being dropped.

On the other hand, positive traditional associations benefited Austria in 2000, when prominent far-right politician Jörg Haider came to power. Austria was able to ride out the resulting negative image impact, which evoked memories of the Third Reich, thanks to strong favorable associations with Mozart, Salzburg, and the Vienna waltz—thus providing a good example of how a positive positioning can serve as inoculation against negative publicity.

Less feasible is the act of repositioning places that have become, rightly or wrongly, tarnished with a negative image and lack sufficient counterbalancing positive features. Colombia's association with drug production, for example, makes image building almost impossible until this problem is corrected. No amount of good marketing can make up for daily headlines about violent crime, gangs, and drug trafficking.

Similar, though less severe, cases where no amount of marketing can fix a broken product include American rust-belt cities. Urban economist Ed Glaeser believes that larger cities play an unparalleled role in economic growth through their ability to attract skilled workers and spread knowledge through proximity. Virtual place, he says, is no match. On the other hand, Glaeser says that it is probably impossible for cities like Buffalo, New York, which has risen and fallen in response to changing transportation technologies and geographic advantages relative to other cities, to ever get out of its downward spiral. All the billions of redevelopment dollars spent to revitalize Buffalo as a place are destined to fail.[12]

Successful Execution of Place Positioning

The most successful instances of place positioning tend to share several features. These include continuity and commitment from top officials, public-private partnerships, connecting the dots, tracking performance, and sustained effort over time. In addition, for nations, there is often a small-country advantage.

In terms of commitment from top officials, there are several benefits to having the head of government of a country or locality invest (without necessarily publicly announcing it) time and political capital in the marketing of a place. First, it underscores the importance to government agencies of following through on plans. Second, this personal involvement in promoting the place impresses the heads of companies contemplating investments. Through countless one-on-one meetings at World Economic Forum events and other venues in the 1980s and 1990s, former Prime Minister Mahathir Mohamad elevated the visibility of Malaysia among multinationals making foreign direct investments. Third, this high level of commitment is needed to motivate the citizenry—including the business, arts, and sports communities—to walk the talk, and deliver on the promise that the chosen positioning strategy makes to the outside world. Despite the potency of electronic communications in the global village, it is, in the final analysis, the quality of personal one-on-one interactions that forms the most lasting perceptions of a place. A place that can persuade its own citizens to live, breathe, and project an authentic image, consistent with its desired positioning, will maximize the impact of its marketing efforts.

The most successful initiatives to secure international sports events, promote exports, and attract outside investment usually involve public-private partnerships. Without private sponsorships, the costs of holding the Olympic Games would be prohibitive for cities. ProChile—an agency cofounded by the Chilean government and the private sector—has for more than thirty years worked closely with government and businesses to establish trade agreements, develop export markets, and attract foreign investment. In selling Chile to new foreign direct investors, the agency leveraged word-of-mouth endorsements from foreign companies that had invested there already; satisfied customers are often the best salespeople.

At the city level, fifty years ago, Atlanta, Georgia, and Birmingham, Alabama, were similar in size and importance as railroad hubs in the South. But during the Civil Rights era, Atlanta began to move ahead by forming a coalition of business and political leaders who joined in promoting the city as a tolerant, pro-business and progressive place. Banding around the catchphrase "the city too busy to hate," private- and public-sector organizations supported a series of major expansions of what has become one of the world's busiest hub airports. Birmingham, meanwhile, became a center of violent unrest, dominated by racist politicians like public safety commissioner Bull Connor. Mired in segregation and discrimination—and lacking the visionary private and public leadership displayed by Atlanta—Birmingham fell behind Atlanta, which now has among the largest concentrations of Fortune 500 companies in the nation.

Because outsiders tend to combine their various exposures and interactions with a place into one overall impression—good, bad, or indifferent—paying attention to as many aspects of the customer experience as possible can be an important source of differential advantage. If the whole of a place's marketing efforts is to be greater than the sum of the parts, the different parties involved must pull together to connect the dots. The speed and ease with which a foreigner can enter the country, the welcome given by an immigration officer, and the modernity of the airport can all make a powerful positive impression on the first-time visitor. The national airline must work with the tourism board; those promoting exports must work with those promoting inward investment; and national marketing must be coordinated with city and regional marketing. Messages reaching different target audiences should be coordinated and consistent, for these various audiences are distinct but not separate: Tourists at today's Olympic Games may be tomorrow's business investors. Conceivably, the champion for connecting the dots could be a mayor or a cabinet minister or agency chief charged with developing a consistent umbrella communications strategy under which campaigns by individual departments reinforce, rather than contradict, each other. In Spain, the Ministry for Industry, Tourism, and Trade is a government organization responsible for marketing the nation overseas, promoting Spanish exports, and attracting inward investment.

The best managed programs track performance as the marketing program progresses, using places that are similarly sized or that are trying to attract the same targets as bases for comparison. Working toward strong rankings on international scorecards, such as the World Economic Forum (WEF) Global Competitiveness Report and the European Commission's Innovation Scoreboard, can also be valuable. Chile, for instance, publicized its rise on the WEF Competitiveness Index. Whether targeting a prospective tourist or business investor, a place needs to achieve the top-of-mind awareness necessary to at least get on the buyer's short list—and for the right reasons. But not at all costs: it is essential to track the economic results of marketing investments and to adjust the allocations against different target groups accordingly. For example, during the 1990s, the United Kingdom found that a million pounds spent promoting foreign direct investment had almost six times the economic multiplier impact than the same amount spent promoting British exports.

Perhaps a more surprising factor is the small-country advantage. Effective nation-state marketing depends on stakeholders having a common cause and rallying around the chosen positioning. In smaller nations, there is often more homogeneity of the citizenry, and consequently, more convergence of views. The need to pull together is often more obvious; to help matters, the political and business elites generally know each other and can more easily formulate a common policy. They may be better able to come to agreement on what constitutes the nation's competitive advantage, which leads to a clear, consistent positioning and mutual reinforcement. The president of the South Korean company Samsung, for instance, participated in advertising campaigns to attract investors to the country. In newly independent states, such as Slovenia or

Croatia, a sense of national purpose can underpin a worldwide marketing effort—particularly when a country is, in economic development terms, ahead of others in the same region and therefore keen to develop a distinct identity.

Whether a place is large or small, improving an image requires sustained effort over time. Postwar Japan achieved its reputation improvement over a thirty-year period, concomitant with investing in new approaches to quality manufacturing. Japan is continuing on this path with R&D investments in robotics. South Korea, like Japan, went through a sustained reputational improvement: first, manufacturing cheap knockoffs, and eventually making Hyundai cars equivalent to Japan's Toyotas, and Samsung televisions as good as Sony's. Now China is on the same trajectory. Clearly, in China's case, there are political issues that bear upon the country's reputation, regardless of product quality. But China's vast talent pool, the emphasis on educational achievement, and increasing opportunity for women will boost China's aspirations to be known as a powerhouse in R&D and innovation.

Place Branding Versus Corporate Branding

While managing a place image is similar in principle to managing a corporate brand, the marketing challenges facing places and corporations do differ in several respects. First, although positioning and messaging can be adapted to target audiences, the climate, history, and culture of a place are what they are. Places are less flexible than brands. The product formula, if you like, cannot be adapted from one country to another as it can with Nescafé or toothpaste.

Second, control over brand or image is often more diffuse. If the place is a nation, local governors and mayors, along with their bureaucracies, will not necessarily pull in the same direction as the national leadership. For example, they will often want to promote their regions and cities more than the nation as a whole, especially when the nation, as in the case of the United Kingdom, is frequently identified overseas with a single world-class city like London. In this case, it becomes difficult for the central government to rally resources behind a single, integrated national campaign. Likewise, if the place is a town, the local council will not necessarily agree on the need for marketing or on the direction it should take. The CEO of a company is better able to develop a joined-up marketing program because even if different division heads want to go their own way, he or she has final say over strategy and the power to allocate resources.

Third, when undertaking marketing campaigns to position or reposition a product or corporate brand image, it is easier for the corporate CEO to enlist the support of employees than for a governmental leader to enlist the support of the public, civil servants, and other stakeholder groups. The CEO pays employees to follow the strategy; if they cannot in conscience do so, they are invited to leave. But a political leader in a democracy has only the power of persuasion to rely on in trying to motivate a broad coalition of citizenry and stake-holder groups to follow a marketing program. If the vast majority of citizens do not buy into, or are cynical about, the marketing proposition, it simply will not work. Outside visitors will discover that the reality does not reflect the promise; such a disconnect can only lead to disappointment, low repeat purchase rates, and negative word of mouth.

Marketing Place Along with Product

Place marketing affects more than just those in the tourism and development industries. Marketers of consumer goods can benefit directly from positive associations with places related to their brand. As we discussed in Chapter 1, place of origin is a strong determinant of consumer choice in certain product categories. Ever since humans began trading goods and services with one another, certain places have developed a reputation based on the products they export. Damascus lends its name to fine steel, China to porcelain, and Madras to a distinctive cloth. Even in today's globally integrated econ-omy, with its emphasis on worldwide sourcing, consumers still associate individual countries, cities, or regions with expertise in particular product categories—whether it is German automobiles, Milanese men's fashions, or French perfumes. Localism, in particular, is increasingly relevant in food marketing. "Massachusetts grown . . . and fresher!" is the slogan for a state initiative that encompasses growers, aquaculturists, retail markets, and restaurants to boost esteem and consumer demand for the state's products, and to develop culinary tourism. In 2010, for example, Massachusetts' demand for local turkeys for the Thanksgiving table rose despite the birds' higher prices and the recession's strain on consumer wallets.[13]

In other product categories as well, there remains a robust percentage of consumers who value doing business with local merchants, in part as a way to support the local economy. For local downtowns that want to reach these consumers, social networking sites have proved to be a boon. Over the 2010 big post-Thanksgiving shopping weekend, American Express (which, of course, profits from increasing the number of merchant transactions) along with Facebook promoted "Small Business Saturday" to boost spending with local merchants. The following Tuesday, Facebook ran a full-page ad in the *New York Times* thanking people for participating and encouraging continued shopping at small local businesses. Governors of Kentucky, New Jersey, New York, Oregon, and Utah, as well as elected officials in other places, joined in the promotion of the event.[14]

Place can become part of the brand identity of business enterprises, and commercial locations can be marketed as destinations. Ads for the Saturn division of General Motors made frequent mention of the location of its assembly plant in Spring Hill, Tennessee, as part of marketing the brand as "a different kind of car company" and to emphasize its independence from its Detroit-based parent. Capitalizing on Scandinavian countries' identification with the clean, simple lines of modern furniture and avoidance of ostentation, IKEA often refers to its Swedish origins and incorporates the Swedish flag in its logo. Real Madrid's iconic Bernabéu Stadium attracts millions of visitors each year. Fans from around the world who cannot attend a game can nevertheless make the pilgrimage to Madrid, in the same way that Catholics are drawn to holy shrines such as Lourdes. L.L.Bean, the outdoor clothing retailer, enjoyed a similar mystique. Customers from around the world could order by catalog but could only see the actual merchandise displayed in the single flagship store, in Freeport, Maine. The store, accommodatingly, stayed open twenty-four hours a day and acquired an aura as a unique destination for casual shoppers and sportsmen. Not until 1992, eighty years after its founding, did the company open a store outside of Maine. Similarly, the Harvard Business School has always resisted temptations to establish sister campuses outside the United States and thereby potentially dilute its brand. Even if additional campuses were established in Asia and Europe, students from these regions would still aspire to go to Boston for the genuine Harvard experience.[15]

In the best of circumstances, associations between brands and places are mutually symbiotic. High-quality brands can lend their luster to the places where they are designed or manufactured, and a better regarded place of origin can in turn benefit manufacturers and brands. With L.L.Bean as the hub, Freeport, Maine, established itself as an outlet center; the additional retail traffic helps drive shoppers to the Bean store. Hyundai contributes to the image of Korea as a place of quality manufacturing and that helps the Samsung and Kia brands. Singapore Airlines creates positive associations with Singapore hospitality, while Singapore's reputation for modernity and efficiency contributes to consumer confidence in the airline's safety and smooth operations. Similarly, in the industrial sector, the success of Embraer, the world's third largest aircraft manufacturer, has bolstered Brazil's status as an emerging economic power, and can be expected to enhance the status of other Brazil-made products.

IBM's "Smarter Cities Challenge" is an interesting example of a multinational corporation seeking to improve its competitive positioning and image by forming associations with cities around the world. The $50 million 3-year program was set up to award competitive grants to 100 cities to make them smarter in using technology to improve education, healthcare, water and energy use, public safety, transportation, and government.[16] The program was a natural follow-on to IBM's "Smarter Planet" campaign, which also emphasized efficiency and sustainability in that an increasing percentage of GDP is concentrated in cities, and sustainable cities are vital to a sustainable planet. Widespread impact was possible in that learning can be transferred among cities: a large city has more in common with another, even across national borders, than with rural areas in the same country. In addition to social responsibility objectives, the campaign gave IBM multiple opportunities to demonstrate its capabilities and to be seen as a trusted local partner in solving urban problems, rather than being perceived as a remote, faceless global enterprise.

The Case of the USA Brand

No place, however well known, can afford to take its image for granted. Since esteem drives attitudes and behaviors, a place that is widely recognized but not liked is poised for a downward slide. In the period following World War II, the United States assumed a preeminent role in the world. Backed by a majority of its politicians and citizens, the nation aspired to be a powerful leader and also one respected for its actions, policies, and values. By and large, foreign citizens and governments admired the country for its international leadership, which combined military strength with soft power; the ethos of the "American Dream," with its core values of democracy and the promise of a better life for all; and its economic success that accounted for more than one-fourth of world GDP.

But recently, thanks to the highly unpopular war in Iraq, revulsion over treatment of prisoners at Abu Ghraib and Guantánamo Bay, and the deep recession hitting the global economy as a result of questionable U.S. financial practices, under the administration of President George W. Bush, the United States' positive image declined precipitously on all three dimensions. Citizens in other nations lost respect for the country, and, as a result, their political leaders gained more latitude in publicly questioning or opposing the United

States. Polls taken by the Pew Research Center in 2008 revealed that positive views of the United States had fallen far below the levels polls reported in 1999 and 2000.[17] A poll commissioned by the BBC World Service in 2007 also yielded bleak results showing that among twenty-six thousand people questioned across the twenty-five largest countries, more than 52 percent thought the United States had a "mostly negative" influence on the world.[18] (See Figure 11.)

On the positive side, most of these negative images were associated with the U.S. government and U.S. leaders, not the American people or American democracy.[19] Although much of the world rejected most of the policies of the Bush administration, there remained a desire for a reformed America to play an important, cooperative role in dealing with global problems. U.S. humanitarian assistance in Africa, including public-health measures, was appreciated; American technologies and products were admired. The cumulative goodwill that the United States—and the values it historically stands for—had built up over generations helped inoculate individual Americans against an immediate backlash. In addition, American multinationals, from McDonald's to IBM, had long worked hard to build local goodwill; however, growing antipathy toward America was giving them cause for worry.

The election of President Barack Obama in 2008 presented an opportunity to wipe the slate clean of the previous administration's perceived failings. The task was immeasurably aided by the convergence of the new leader's image with positively viewed aspects of the country. Obama personified such

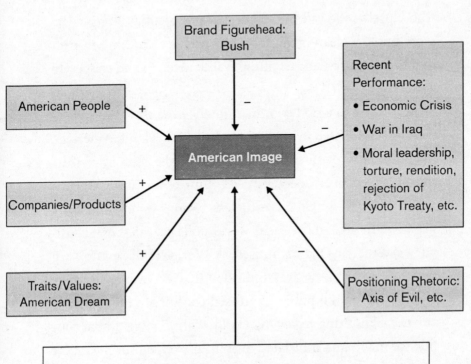

FIGURE 11. Reshaping America's Image

core American values as hope, opportunity, tolerance, and community, and to the millions of people around the world who closely followed the American presidential election, he represented a clean break from the past, a refreshing respect for other cultures, and a willingness to listen to and cooperate with others.

According to a poll commissioned by the BBC World Service and conducted by the University of Maryland, America's image improved immediately following the election.[20] (The survey polled 13,575 people in 26 countries for 10 weeks, ending February 1, 2009.) Nevertheless, ratings were still mainly negative, though subsequent world polls revealed extraordinary esteem for Obama himself. A WorldPublicOpinion.org poll, released in July 2009, indicated that, on average, 61 percent of the foreign public expressed confidence in Obama to "do the right thing regarding world affairs." High global confidence in Obama translated to an improvement in the image of the United States, which nevertheless lagged well behind confidence in the president and left considerable room for further improvement.[21]

The upturn in America's global image also stemmed in part from a combination of relief that the Bush administration's tone and policies were gone, and, importantly, from active image management by the new administration. Obama deliberately and quickly moved to signal changed intentions and a new tone. Reflecting the priority on foreign audiences, the president made five overseas trips, visiting fourteen countries, within the first six months of taking office. During the first trip—to the G20 and NATO summits, followed by a symbolically important visit to predominantly Muslim Turkey—Obama's frequently repeated message that America needed to respect and partner with other nations was well received. During a widely reported town hall meeting in Strasbourg, France, the president apologized for the deterioration of relationships with European nations, while also talking about the problem as a two-way street. A major speech delivered in Cairo, in the heart of the Arab world, was aimed at bridging divisions between Islamic countries and the West.

The State Department, which is formally in charge of America's image, explored new ways to reach out to the foreign public consistent with the new positioning of American world leadership. U.S. embassies had at one time hosted cultural centers where foreign citizens could absorb positive aspects of American life; but due to threats of terrorist attacks, embassies were transformed into fortified bunkers where foreigners were unwelcome. To replace the centers, the State Department's public diplomacy office has experimented with a new high-tech, interactive facility called @America. Significantly, rather than expecting people who were lukewarm at best toward the United States to make a special trip to the center, a trial version was set up in a shopping mall in Jakarta, Indonesia, which made the enterprise more accessible to the intended audience of young Muslims.[22] Of course, the State Department will need to ensure that actions back up such outreach to foreign publics—for example, making it easier to get a visa and monitoring how immigration officials interrogate visitors.

Repositioning the American brand depends on sustained commitment; of utmost importance, U.S. actions must be consistent with its rhetoric. If not undermined by a disconnect between acts and words, indicators of the success of the Obama repositioning would include a replenishment of the reservoir of goodwill toward the U.S. government, its people, and American companies and brands held by foreign publics historically favorable toward the United States. Another indicator would be an improvement in the negative attitudes held by foreign publics historically hostile toward the United States. Still another would be the impact of the repositioning on the internal audience: that is, a shift in the American public's views of its relationships with other countries—toward a preference for policies characterized by mutual respect and partnership and away from a preference for unilateral leadership.

The case of "brand USA" illustrates a number of points relevant to the marketing of both place and products. One is that a long-held overall favorable image can offer protection against negative one-off events—such as a product-safety recall or a despised policy. Another is that brand images influence place image, and vice versa. The storehouse of goodwill toward American brands—accumulated partly as a result of historically favorable attitudes toward America—mediated anti-U.S. sentiment; but such protective effects cannot last forever. The case also illustrates the role of leadership in connecting the dots and ensuring that image is congruent with the reality of the product or place.

In general, place and physical context still remain powerful means for commercial marketers to communicate brand attributes. While any product can be shipped around the world, the place-based heritage of the brand can still determine sales success. We are not saying that all brands have a reason to highlight their place of origin, but we do believe that all companies need to be aware of their favorable and unfavorable place-based associations—and seek to improve the negative associations wherever possible. Next, we turn our attention to the challenge of being both global and local, and the ways in which multinational marketers can leverage market leadership in a home country into multiple local successes around the world.

Chapter 5

MARKETING LOCALLY AND GLOBALLY

Ever since Theodore Levitt penned his famous *Harvard Business Review* paper, "The Globalization of Markets," in 1983, the question of whether and how far to adapt a global brand's marketing program to the needs and nuances of local markets has been hotly contested. Levitt argued, "The global competitor will seek constantly to standardize his offerings everywhere. He will digress from this standardization only after exhausting all possibilities to retain it, and he will push for reinstatement of standardization whenever digression and divergence have occurred. He will never assume that the customer is a king who knows his own wishes."[1] In the intervening years, we have seen that the answer to the standardization question typically varies by product category (for instance, do customer tastes for products in the category vary from country to country?) and by country market (does management in the country have the skills and resources to develop optimal marketing approaches? For example, in the early 1990s when Eastern European countries opened up to the West, multinationals required entrepreneurial managers to seize opportunities in these evolving and expanding markets. Instead, what many had was bureaucratic managers who lacked the political savvy and flexibility to take appropriate action.).

The back-and-forth debate, global versus local, reminds us that the pendulum is moving fastest when it passes through the midpoint. The search for balance between global and local may be illusory, but these days we believe that the best global brands—from IBM to McDonald's—are the best local brands, and vice versa. Such brands bring global quality and innovation to local markets while drawing on local ideas and insights about a brand's use to help build sales in different markets around the globe.

Parallel to the localization decisions discussed in Chapter 2, the degree to which a brand decides to adapt internationally should be managed on a case-by-case basis. If the extra costs, in time and money, of adapting a marketing program are more than covered through higher unit prices or more sales at the same price, adaptation may be worth it. But if the important factor of speed of rollout in determining a new product's success trumps local market customization, then it is not. And the technical resources that might go into local adaptation may best be focused on bringing the next new product to market earlier.

Regardless, chief marketing officers of major multinationals have to strive simultaneously for excellence in local and global marketing. Developing home-grown marketers with local consumer knowledge—who at the same time are open to ideas from other countries—remains the best way to ensure that the global brand stays strong at the local level. The best marketing people master the art of choosing the appropriate scale or scales for each type of marketing decision and linking the local to the global, the psychological place to the physical and virtual place.

From Local to Global

The slogan of HSBC—"The World's Local Bank"—perfectly captures the dual requirements for companies with international or global aspirations. To be a strong global player, you have to be a strong local player. In the world of high-stakes banking, being perceived as local may seem of little significance, but the global and the local run in tandem for two reasons: local customers believe they are getting access to cutting-edge services if they are with a global bank, while global clients want to believe that the bank really understands their local conditions and specific needs.

The odds of success in global markets are daunting. Usually, successful ventures require large investments of human and/or financial capital, the willingness to risk multiple failed attempts, and the patience to wait years for profits to materialize. So another reason that top global brands are also outstanding local brands is that a company typically has to build a strong presence—with accompanying cash flows—in its home market before it can expand globally. However, even the best brands have trouble dominating in new markets. Google, despite its global recognition, is far behind the market leaders for Internet search engines Yandex and Baidu, in Russia and China, respectively. Yandex holds about a 64 percent market share of searches in Russia versus 22 percent for Google; likewise, in 2009, Baidu held about a 64 percent share of searches in China versus 31 percent for Google.

U.S. and Japanese firms exemplify two different bases for a strong home market. Thanks to the huge size and vigorous competition of the U.S. domestic consumer market, leading American companies were well equipped—in terms of access to risk capital and marketing skills, in the last decade of the twentieth century—to invest and compete overseas. After the end of the Cold War, for example, Coca-Cola formed Coca-Cola Refreshments-Moscow—one of the early private-sector companies owned by a foreign multinational corporation in Russia—in order both to manufacture soft-drink syrups as well as set up a retail distribution network, which required training a sales force.[2] General Electric made one of the first significant investments in Eastern Europe with its purchase of Hungarian lighting company Tungsram—and had to wait four years to turn a profit.

Significantly, leading national brands in the United States are accustomed to fighting hard for every point of market share in local geographies. A brand that is number one nation-ally may be number two or three or four in many individual localities. Even Coke and Pepsi experience significant differ-ences in market share depending on whether you are looking at Louisville or Las Vegas.[3] This experience helps to prepare U.S. national marketers to compete in global markets where, likewise, the objective is often to assemble a dominant market-share position across fragmented geographies.

Alternatively, Japanese firms benefit from "Japan, Inc."—an interconnected constellation of government ministries, financial institutions, and trading companies with a concen-trated focus on exporting high-value goods to affluent foreign markets—and home-market protectionism whereby the gov-ernment adopts isolationist policies hindering foreign imports and businesses in favor of Japanese businesses.[4] Supported by these policies, Toyota, Sony, and Canon are among the top global brands. Japanese firms have been less well equipped to compete in marketing smaller-ticket items to less affluent countries. Shiseido, whose cosmetics and skin-care products lead other foreign brands in China, is one of the few excep-tions. Shiseido's founder had modeled the company after Western-style pharmacies when he started it in 1872, and management early on gradually expanded the brand into new markets: it exported first to Asian countries in the 1930s and then in the early 1960s entered Hawaii, where there is a large Japanese-American population. Currently, low growth oppor-tunities in the home market continue to fuel Shiseido's global ambitions.[5]

Market Expansion Strategies

There are two alternative approaches to geographic expansion: simultaneous versus waterfall. Each may be appropriate, depending on circumstances.

Simultaneous

The simultaneous (or near simultaneous) national or worldwide strategy usually carries higher risk and is harder to organize. But rapid and preemptive action can pay off where the cost of delay exceeds the cost of chaos. Starting in the early 1990s, Nokia expanded quickly into world markets from its home base in Finland and today holds a third of the global market share for mobile telephones, with sales in more than 150 countries. Its lead was facilitated by its participation in developing the dominant Global System for Mobile communication (GSM) second-generation mobile technology, which was adopted as the standard for telecommunications in Europe and by carriers in many other countries. As the market for mobile phones soared, Nokia offered inexpensive but high-quality phones for the masses as well as fancier phones with additional features for higher-end consumers. In particular, the company scored early successes in Asia, South America, and North America.

A simultaneous global rollout strategy is also used by Microsoft in launching new generations of operating systems in order to establish a preemptive standard for software that applies worldwide. Moreover, the time and monetary costs in terms of customizing operating-system software for individual countries—other than essential language adaptations—would be prohibitive and would divert development resources from the next-generation upgrade. Simultaneous global expansion allows companies to gain a quick competitive advantage over competitors in a lot of different markets at once. Similar consumer needs across a wide range of geographies and adequate distribution systems in other markets are existing conditions that also favor this approach.

On the other hand, an overly aggressive push by management and shareholders for expansion from local to subnational, national, or global coverage can endanger the core business. The case of the casual-dining Boston Market chain (formerly Boston Chicken) offers a cautionary tale of too-hasty expansion. Founded in 1985, the company quickly grew to fourteen outlets in the Boston area and was bought and taken public six years later by two former Blockbuster executives who relocated headquarters to Chicago. The new management launched an ambitious drive to expand nationally through franchisees. After buying back franchise stores for hundreds of millions of dollars and undergoing restructuring, the company went into bankruptcy in 1998, from which it was only rescued by a sale to McDonald's in 2000. Boston Market was later sold to a private equity firm when McDonald's decided to refocus on its core hamburger business.

Although Starbucks is in much better shape, its drive for rapid national and international expansion also resulted in too many stores in some geographical areas as well as deterioration of customer service in existing stores. Moreover, the justification for Starbucks' premium prices became jeopardized by the brand's geographical ubiquity, which reduced the perceived exclusivity of the brand. With the 2008 financial crisis further reducing the appeal of four-dollar lattes, the company ended up closing three hundred stores. The company's insistence on aggressive expansion is interesting given that a circa 2000 analysis of its U.S. growth strategy concluded that the company could have met yearly cash goals while cutting investments nearly by half if it had built about a third fewer stores—picking those with the highest potential profit contribution and taking into account not just the incremental value of a new store but also the impact on the value of the stores around it.[6]

Waterfall

The opposite of the simultaneous strategy is the waterfall, an incremental city-by-city or country-by-country approach to market expansion that has many variants. Generally, even in today's global economy, neighboring countries are still one another's biggest trading partners—such as Canada and Mexico for the United States; France and other members of the European Union for Germany. So one approach to going international is to establish beachheads in those neighboring countries first—where there is likely more familiarity with the brand and where brand marketers can more easily gauge consumer tastes—and set up distribution systems. Though a short geographical distance does not always mean a short cultural distance, a short supply chain usually serves to mitigate risk, and a more controlled approach allows you to enter adjacent markets quickly.

Factors that favor this approach include a varying degree of category or brand presence, or competitive activity between regions; different local government regulations and laws that impact the business model; and a preference for local adaptation rather than standardization among consumers. With a waterfall expansion companies should start with geographically contiguous areas and identify clusters of countries that share important characteristics with established markets.

Serving geographically contiguous areas or geographically concentrated customers may also be an important component of a competitive strategy because of low costs. Southwest Airlines, for example, started with service to the Dallas-Houston-San Antonio triangle in Texas from a home base at Love Field, located outside Dallas, operating on the principle of "Meet customers' short-haul travel needs at fares competitive with the cost of automobile travel." Thus, as it became a national airline, its strategy remained based upon a low-cost, low-fare standard. Another factor that shaped its growth strategy was geographical restrictions imposed by government agencies. In 1971, competitors persuaded Congress to limit Southwest's operations to Texas; then national carriers successfully lobbied Congress to prevent flights from Love Field to all but contiguous states, a restriction that was not eased until 2006.[7] Although Southwest's circumstances are unique, legal and regulatory conditions are frequently relevant when deciding where to expand.

Another variant of the waterfall approach is to enter a cluster of countries that may be geographically distant but which share important characteristics. In the 1990s the South Korean company Samsung decided to transition its core business strategy away from being an original equipment manufacturer of cheap televisions for other brand names to becoming a high-value-added marketer of premium-priced consumer electronics products under a strong global brand name. To carry out the transition, it adopted a rollout approach, whereby it focused on emerging markets first (where loyalties to established brands were less deep-rooted and where there were higher percentages of young people whose brand loyalties were up for grabs) and tackled tough-to-enter developed markets later. Samsung is now the world's largest consumer-electronics brand. The Chinese automaker Chery—which turned out its first vehicle in 1999, based on a Volkswagen-licensed chassis—is taking a similar approach. In addition to becoming the most successful domestically branded auto company in China, Chery has started exporting to bellwether markets in developing countries; as of this writing, it has its sights set on entering developed markets in the United States and Europe, competing with the big six American and Japanese automakers.[8]

When it comes to the larger of the fast-growth emerging economies—among them the four "BRIC" countries of Brazil, Russia, India, and China—most multinational marketers should not treat any of them as single national markets. The countries are too large and too heterogeneous. In either the focus or beachhead strategies shown in Figure 12, marketers address a few local markets within a country. In the beachhead strategy, the aim is to establish an initial foothold in a

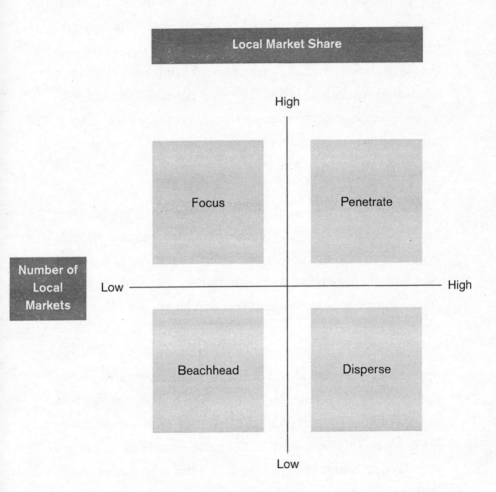

FIGURE 12. Strategies for Geographic Expansion Within Large, Fast-Growing Countries

new market. In the focus strategy, the aim is to achieve a high share of a selected local market. In a growing market like China, sticking with the focus strategy of "skimming the cream" of affluent Western-oriented consumers in the tier-one cities provides low-risk revenues but insufficient growth opportunities by ignoring vast swathes of the population. Instead, marketers committed to increasing their national market share need a geographic rollout strategy similar to that used to penetrate the vast geography of the United States a hundred years ago: Start in the major cities and, with beach-heads established, proceed to the disperse (seek a market share in many market areas) or penetrate (aim for high market share in many markets) strategies among second- and third-tier cities. In these cities, less experienced consumers may need to be educated about product functionality and benefits, and less affluent consumers may require simpler product versions or smaller sizes. But, as per capita incomes rise, households pass trigger points where they will start consuming more products—from soft drinks to cars—that were once out of their reach.

Part of McDonald's penetration strategy in China is to open retail locations ahead of the demand curve; this allows the company to preempt the competition by securing the best local franchise partners and the best high-traffic locations at lower costs. This early-bird strategy also enables the company to establish brand recognition at a time when advertising costs are low and competitors are few.

Other options for waterfall expansion are to buy or partner

with existing firms in one or more markets. Here you can gain complementarity in geographic coverage, as is common in airline industry alliances. You can also quickly acquire the expertise of local employees, access to distribution, and established brand presence. The Chinese appliance maker Haier has successfully entered new markets—often niche markets—in more than 160 countries via a series of joint ventures and partnerships. Henkel and other industrial companies use independent, exclusive distributors to open up international markets, then buy them out when they achieve a sales volume sufficient to warrant a direct sales organization or a system of multiple, competing distributors. A company with distribution strength in one region may purchase a second company with strengths in a different region. If the two companies manufacture complementary products in the same category, there is an opportunity to now sell the entire line in both geographies. Such potential geographical synergies are often important in calculating and justifying an acquisition price in mergers and acquisitions.

However, the acquisition or partnership approach often fails to cultivate the parent company's brand name and may result in a hard-to-manage patchwork of operations that cannot easily be scaled up to expand into additional markets. For instance, Quaker Oats, which already owned Gatorade, acquired Snapple in 1994 to build a critical mass of beverage brands. Quaker Oats marketed Gatorade mostly in the southern United States, in supermarkets, while Snapple sold mostly to convenience stores through a network of about three hundred small, independent distributors in the Northeast. On paper, the product and geographic synergies stemming from the acquisition looked convincing. In reality, when Quaker attempted to integrate distribution channels, negotiations with Snapple distributors failed. Further, unlike Gatorade, Snapple sold best in single-serving sizes rather than multiunit packs. Gatorade-style large packs took up too much retail display space in convenience stores, and Snapple-style single bottles with many flavor variations were less efficient for supermarkets. Moreover, Snapple's quirky brand personality proved to be a poor fit with the more buttoned-down Quaker, which sold the brand at a loss three years later. Similarly, the Chinese firm TCL Multimedia's acquisition of television assets from the French company Thomson has not worked well. TCL hoped that marrying low-cost manufacturing with an established sales and marketing structure and brand would create synergistic returns, but integrating Chinese and French management proved much more difficult than expected.

Adapting to Multiple Geographies

Once a company or brand has entered a market, how can it fit the need to be a good local marketer into the overall marketing plan? This is a broader question than the familiar debate over adaptation versus standardization in international marketing. The latter tends to focus on adaptation versus standardization of the marketing mix—that is, whether or not to use the same branding, products, positioning, pricing, and methods of distribution—whereas the former includes country management as well. A useful tool for addressing such questions is the type of planning grid depicted in Figure 13.

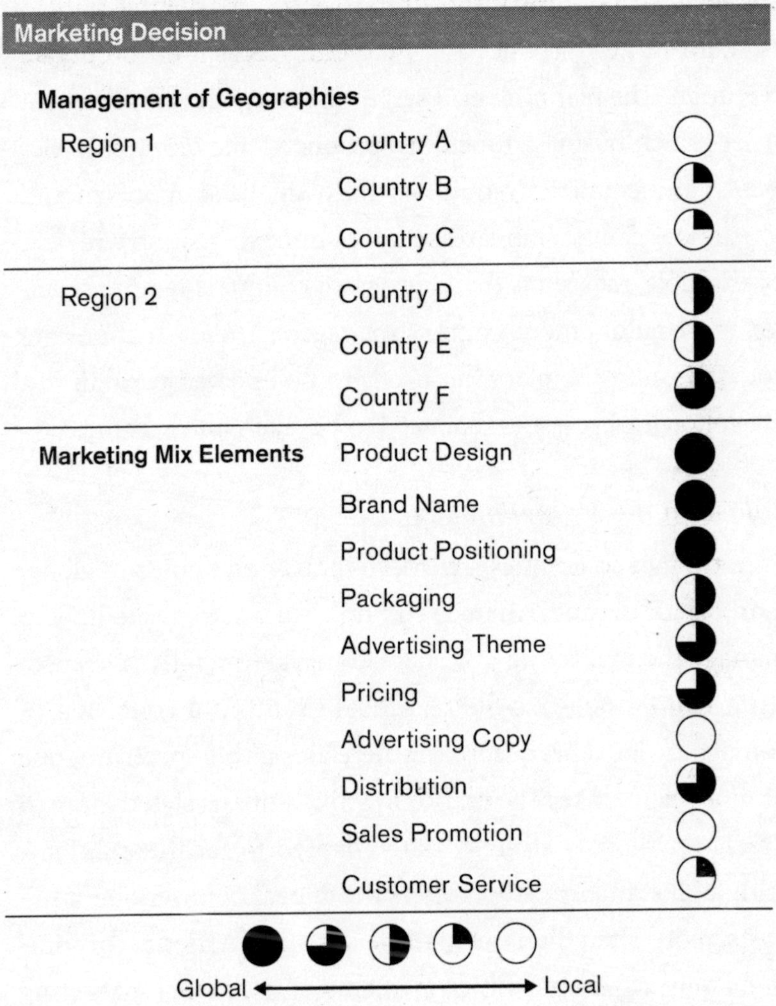

Marketing Decision		
Management of Geographies		
Region 1	Country A	○
	Country B	◔
	Country C	◔
Region 2	Country D	◐
	Country E	◐
	Country F	◕
Marketing Mix Elements	Product Design	●
	Brand Name	●
	Product Positioning	●
	Packaging	◐
	Advertising Theme	◕
	Pricing	◕
	Advertising Copy	○
	Distribution	◕
	Sales Promotion	○
	Customer Service	◔

● ◕ ◐ ◔ ○

Global ⟵⟶ Local

FIGURE 13. Example of Planning Grid for Geographic Scale of Marketing Decisions

Take Company X, which has historically been quite decentralized and where local managers have had considerable autonomy; but now the company is in the process of concentrating decision-making power at headquarters. As part of this process, it is conferring more authority on central marketing staff to standardize new product and marketing ideas and coordinate execution. The planning grid serves the company as a checklist to see which business functions, products, marketing mix elements, and countries require an individualized approach and which ones can be standardized. A country-by-country review, for example, may show that one or two countries require stronger, more autonomous country managers. These situations are not static, and the planning needs to be updated periodically. The following are issues that need to be taken into account.

Adjusting the Marketing Mix

Even though companies have been managing brands in global markets for decades, there is still no clear answer as to how to manage the marketing mix. Global marketing falls on a spectrum from a one-size-fits-all global brand to a collection of completely local brands; somewhere along this spectrum, one or more elements of the marketing mix—often related more to execution than to strategy—are adapted to local conditions. Although standardization offers the appeal of lower operating costs, more often than not managers in multinational corporations must figure out which elements of the global marketing concept to tailor to local conditions and how to make the added complexities pay out in extra profitability. In general, even if the strategy and brand name is globally standardized, the execution of promotional programs, channel selection, sales, and customer service must be largely localized.

Global brands enjoy many advantages. They signal product quality, and while in some cases consumers may prefer a distinctly local look and feel in products they buy, these attributes are not incompatible with a global brand name.[9] In fact, consumers sometimes mistake what is actually a global brand for a local brand. In a recent survey of urban Chinese consumers, for example, 90 percent thought Tide was a local brand.[10] And while Samsung dominated the South Korean domestic market, it used to downplay its Korean heritage in international markets—before it (and companies such as Hyundai and LG) became associated with high quality. As a result, many consumers still think it is a global Japanese brand.

Global brands are also able to leverage their marketing communications. Only they, for example, can afford the global sponsorship costs associated with the Olympics or World Cup soccer. These events have become so important in brand marketing that sponsorship of them enables brands to distance themselves further from their nearest rivals. The fact that Coca-Cola has the benefit of being the exclusive sponsor of both these events helps to explain why Pepsi trails Coca-Cola in almost every international market.

The most valuable global brands, as measured by annual rankings by Interbrand and Millward Brown's BrandZ, display a single-minded product category focus. Microsoft means software; Nokia means cell phones; Google means search.

When a brand name comes close to "owning" a category, it becomes very powerful. In addition, since the product and corporate brands are one and the same, there are cost efficiencies in developing worldwide brand recognition versus dispersing the marketing budget across the corporate brand plus multiple product brands.

Does it always make sense to develop a global brand? The strategy works well for newer product categories without strong preexisting brand preferences, luxury products, and high-technology products. But what about older product categories for which local customs, tastes, and traditions may have been well established in the preglobal world? Global brands generally command a price premium but there is a limit to the size of the consumer segment willing to pay it. In many cases, global players will want to serve other segments as well, by offering the market a portfolio of brands—some local, some global. In China, for example, the American company Yum! Brands has launched the East Dawning chain of fast-food restaurants, serving Chinese food, to complement its highly successful KFC global brand, which—despite its fast-food aesthetic in the United States—offers sit-in dining for middle-class Chinese consumers in an attractive setting. In the beer category, two global companies, ABInBev and SABMiller, dominate the global playing field but are pursuing different strategies. The category is highly fragmented: the two most international brands, Heineken and Corona, command only 1.5 percent each of the global market, while the leading brand in the world, Snow—with 4 percent market share—is sold only in China. ABInBev, with 19 percent global market share, is trying to establish Budweiser as a global brand similar to Coca-Cola. To reach a global audience, Budweiser invested in sponsoring the 2010 FIFA World Cup, accompanied by an extensive online social media campaign, Internet search ads, and television commercials in twenty countries. Similarly, in China, ABInBev is trying to take Harbin, a regional beer, national. In contrast, SABMiller believes that beer—a product that has been produced for millennia and where some breweries and brands have been around for hundreds of years—is an inherently local product. The company is thus emphasizing the local heritage of the local brands that it has acquired around the world, and is using the work of sociologists, anthropologists, and historians to ascertain the place they occupy in consumers' psychological space. It is pinning fewer hopes on globalizing its flagship Miller brand, although it is on the alert for opportunities to link the meaning of Miller to local cultural references.[11]

If a brand has a strong locational or national association in its profile, then it may not be suitable as a global brand. Such brands must be modified or supplemented or replaced by brands developed for foreign markets. For example, many British companies dropped the "British" from their names as their global sales and operations became more pronounced (for example, British Airports Authority became BAA Limited; British Petroleum became BP; British Aerospace became BAE Systems)—perhaps also to erase associations with colonialism. Inevitably, the 2010 Gulf of Mexico oil spill from a BP drilling rig prompted many journalists to again refer to the company as British Petroleum.

In terms of the product component of the marketing mix, the food category is a good example of one where marketers can offer the same brand worldwide but may need to modify products. KFC offers tempura chicken strips in Japan and changes the formulation of its secret recipe within China—the chicken gets progressively spicier the further inland you move. Coca-Cola is highly standardized in terms of branding, positioning, advertising theme, and Coke flavor, but the sweeteners used in the product formulation and the packaging vary across countries—for example, cane sugar is used in Mexico versus the high-fructose corn syrup in the United States; smaller bottles are sold in rural areas of China to hit a one-renminbi price point. Similarly, in the personal-care category, global toothpaste brands offer different flavors to cater to local consumer preferences: In China, Colgate and Crest hold a combined 50 percent of market share for oral care thanks to locally adapted toothpaste flavors—like salt (Colgate) and tea flavors (Crest). Like product formulas, distribution strategies also call for adaptation by global brands. Hindustan Lever's large distribution network reaches rural areas through mom-and-pop stores, door-to-door sales forces employing local women, and bicycle deliveries to more remote villages to achieve maximum coverage. In many emerging countries, Dell could not export its Internet-based build-to-order approach to selling computers because few end consumers have credit cards to pay with. Dell has therefore had to reembrace traditional distribution methods. In China, the

American direct-selling companies Avon and Mary Kay proved so successful against local competitors that the central government abruptly banned direct selling in the 1990s, forcing the companies to seek distribution through retail outlets. In short, customers, competitive conditions, and government regulations differ from place to place, and therefore few brands can compete at the fully standardized end of the spectrum.

However, marketers should draw the line at tinkering with the core positioning of the brand. A global marketer like Johnson & Johnson, for example, maintains premium pricing everywhere even though it may have to accept lower margins in less-developed countries. J&J also considers how changing the positioning in one market affects the global integrity of its product-line strategy: local revisions may cause delays and disrupt the logical sequence of follow-on product introductions, leading to extra costs and operational complexity.[12]

Integrating Local Expertise into Strategy

Turning to the larger question of what it means for a multinational company to be a good local marketer, one of the big issues is simply marrying global know-how and strategy with local knowledge and cultural grounding. For example, if a particular line of high-end cosmetics has been successful among a certain segment of consumers in France, a cosmetics marketer might be able to identify a segment of consumers within Brazil possessing similar characteristics. Seizing this opportunity may then come down to ensuring that colors are adapted to Brazilian women's skin colorations. In a similar way, local knowledge of Saudi Arabia might then also indicate that, contrary to Western expectations, many women wear high-end cosmetics in their homes and at private parties, making them a good target for the same premium product line. A microsegment in one country might be too small to capture the attention of a global brand, but not if aggregated across 192 nations.

In many emerging economies, reliable market research data is hard to come by, particularly regarding household wealth: consumers don't like to disclose their finances and engage in fewer transactions with financial service firms than do consumers in developed economies. This lack of data puts a premium on access to managers with deep local expertise. Being local also means understanding not just data but prevailing cultural attitudes and political nuances. Google has learned the hard way that European attitudes toward privacy and the Chinese government's policies on censorship mean that it cannot operate in the same way in these markets as it does in its home market. Likewise, being local means having good intelligence on local competition. There are highly resilient, well-managed brands in local markets that are successfully defending themselves against multinational corporations. Consumers may experiment with global brands but then return to favorite local brands—which in many cases improve their quality as a direct response to competitive pressure from global marketers.

Becoming a Good Local Citizen

A crucial aspect of being a good local marketer is being a great local citizen in every market. McDonald's, for example, invests in communities via franchising to local businessmen, training local managers, and contributing to local charities. On a larger geographic scale, it buys local raw materials and recruits local sports stars as endorsers in ads. In many instances the high standards McDonald's holds itself to may force other companies (including local competitors) to improve standards as well. This benefits all citizens in the countries in which it operates.

As noted earlier, citizens' attitudes toward localism are increasingly intertwined with attitudes toward globalism. Caring about the global environment and exploitation of natural resources manifests in consumers' wanting to know where things come from, and how they are manufactured and processed. With regard to sustainable consumption, there is growing agreement that corporations have a critical role to play in innovating business processes and products so as to minimize environmental costs, removing adverse products and services from the marketplace, and using marketing campaigns to educate and encourage consumers to act upon their sustainability beliefs.[13] At Henkel, the German multinational corporation that sells household care, personal care, and adhesive products, "sustainability is a core business factor" and part of the corporate mind-set—as evident in the declaration that "products aligned to the needs of consumers in the lower income brackets not only have enormous economic potential, but also make a positive social contribution in terms of household hygiene, for example, and hence health. We therefore adapt our products to local conditions, different income levels, infrastructures, or cultural needs, so that our performance and our quality are accessible to the broadest possible group of people." Hence, in India, Henkel's Henko brand laundry detergent incorporates a natural raw anti-bacterial ingredient obtained from native Neem trees.[14]

Managing Globally

Juggling the local, the regional, and the global imposes complex demands on the marketing organization in multinational corporations—particularly when customers vary widely in scope and scale. International companies have transitioned through a number of organizational models, but many continue to employ a geographically based structure.

Country-by-Country Management

Historically, controlling international trade required trading companies to assign their own agents and representatives in the most important ports. This approach, essentially an export model, became the model for the international company of the early twentieth century. But, to penetrate a foreign market further, rather than just skimming the surface, it was necessary to establish distribution. Typically, foreign companies would recruit or develop local distributors on an exclusive or nonexclusive basis for a period of years with specific market development goals.

As demand expanded in the foreign market, economies of scale and scope meant that it became prudent for the international company to consider domestic manufacturing, particularly if necessary raw materials could be sourced locally. The international company could then buy out the independent distributorship, absorb its people into its own sales force, and set up a wholly owned subsidiary headed by a country general manager. The result would be a geographically based reporting structure that assigns profit-and-loss responsibility to country or regional managers. It is an especially suitable structure when significant cross-border differences in demand require product formulas or marketing programs to be modified from one country to another. It is also appropriate when there are significant within-country needs for adaptation, as when a company moves beyond a cosmopolitan capital to the rural hinterlands in search of new demand. For example, it may be necessary to adapt by using salespeople on bicycles rather than in vans, or to make product formulas and packaging robust enough to withstand harsher climactic conditions.

Many of today's long-standing multinational corporations in the consumer goods industry—such as Colgate-Palmolive of the United States, Nestlé of Switzerland, and Unilever of the United Kingdom—passed through this pattern of development. To this day, they are structured along geographic lines with country general managers reporting to regional managers reporting to headquarters. These place-based organizations respond to four realities. First, the world comprises 193 sovereign independent nation-states (the number of members of the United Nations) that are defined by geographic boundaries. Second, these nations have their own laws and regulations. Third, they often vary in language, culture, and consumer

preferences. Fourth, they compete for foreign direct investment. If the scale of customer demand is sufficient or growing
rapidly toward sufficiency, it makes sense for Colgate or Nestlé
to invest in a manufacturing plant in that country. A commitment to local manufacturing and a fully staffed country subsidiary may well impress the local political leadership and
result in favorable consideration on government contracts
and other benefits. Pepsi locally sources 99 percent of the
raw material needed for manufacturing in each country—
both because there is local pressure and because it is more
economical.

Transnational Management

However, as the forces of globalization became more prominent from the 1980s onward, the case for country-by-country
management was challenged. Increased travel, decreased telecommunications costs, and satellite television, among other
forces, brought more people from different countries into contact with each other, leading to easier transfers of ideas and
best practices on the management side and greater convergence in preferences on the customer side. Theodore Levitt
observed that consumers everywhere wanted world-class
modernity at economical prices.[15] Even the most patriotic
American could be tempted to buy a globally standardized
Japanese car because the value for money and product quality
appeared simply too good to pass up compared with the locally
produced Chrysler, Ford, and GM alternatives. Perhaps Japanese cars were not completely adapted to American roads, trip

lengths, and interior amenity preferences, but they hit a highly appealing retail price point.

Accordingly, a number of companies moved to a transnational type of organization that attempted to integrate assets and resources across country borders to achieve greater efficiencies and scale economies.[16] Responsibility for profits and losses was assigned to managers of worldwide product categories or strategic business units rather than assigned by geography (see Figure 14). This model was especially appropriate for technology-based products, such as consumer electronics, and almost all business-to-business products, where customers around the world bought largely on the same criteria, weighed the product attributes similarly in relative importance, and made similar feature versus price trade-offs. With increased competition, speedy access to the global market became essential. High-tech companies like Intel and Microsoft turned over their product lines so quickly that they had neither the management time nor research and development resources to adapt to local market preferences, real or imagined. To market such products effectively, a global product director or business unit manager at headquarters could survey the global competitive landscape, spread the best new product ideas quickly around the global network, set up manufacturing plants in a few locations to maximize global supply chain efficiencies, and develop a truly global strategy. The bulk-to-value ratio on technology products is high, so their shipping costs as a percentage of final price could be relatively low, even if shipped worldwide from a single manufacturing plant.

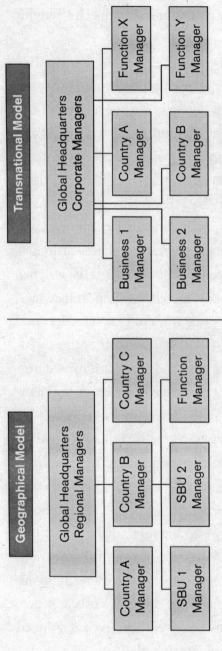

Transnational Model

Global Headquarters
Corporate Managers

- Function X Manager
- Function Y Manager
- Country A Manager
- Country B Manager
- Business 1 Manager
- Business 2 Manager

- Stable markets and political or economic environment
- Compete based on efficiencies from standardization
- Innovation comes from R&D
- Increased control over local markets
- Complex matrix structure

Geographical Model

Global Headquarters
Regional Managers

- Country C Manager
- Function Manager
- Country B Manager
- SBU 2 Manager
- Country A Manager
- SBU 1 Manager

- Emerging markets, uncertain political or economic environment
- Local knowledge and adaptation in order to compete
- Innovation comes from market
- Entrepreneurial local management
- Country potentates

FIGURE 14. Geography-Based Versus Transnational Organizational Models

198

The increased prominence of regional trading blocs further diminished the appeal of the country management system. To counter the economic muscle of the U.S. market, the European Union tightened integration across national boundaries in 1992, with the removal of nontariff barriers to intra-EU trade. By 2010, the EU included 27 member states, whose combined population of over 492 million significantly exceeded the 307 million population of the United States. The North American Free Trade Agreement brought Canada, Mexico, and the United States closer together. Similarly, the Mercosur agreement in Latin America linked Argentina, Brazil, Paraguay, and Uruguay. At one level, these agreements confirmed the power of geography in influencing trade flows. Most countries' leading trading partners (adjusting for size of economy) are their next-door neighbors. At another level, regional integration elevated the power of regional management in multinational corporations at the expense of country managers. Increasingly observable in Scandinavia, a multinational's activities in a small slow-growth country might now be run by a sales manager reporting to a country manager in the neighboring geography, with that organization providing all back-office support.

A Resurgence in Country Management

A scramble to dominate new product markets as quickly as possible was triggered by the opening up, in the 1990s, of various geographies to free-market capitalism. The breakup of the Soviet Union and Yugoslavia, the opening of China, deregulation of the Indian economy, and privatization throughout

Latin America all collectively added 3 billion consumers to the world's free-market economy. Ironically, one result has been a renewed emphasis on country management in global corporations. Having been shielded from the free-market economy, these countries were marked by strong cultural differences affecting consumer preferences. But Western multinationals typically had few senior managers at headquarters who had experience in these countries. Hence there was the need to establish strong country organizations on the ground that could understand the market, develop distribution and sales capabilities to penetrate vast geographies, and show powerful national governments an appropriate level of commitment.

Country management is therefore enjoying a resurgence in multinational companies, at least in the large, fast-growth markets. Many of the emerging economies—the BRIC countries in particular—offer vast market potential at a time when population growth is close to zero and price pressure from excess capacity is squeezing profit margins in most of the developed world. In smaller or slow-growth country markets, the case for country management remains far less persuasive. Thus, the same company may appropriately use different organizational approaches in different parts of the world. In Europe, characterized by slow growth, managers of large business units might report directly to world headquarters. In Asia, where there are significant differences in culture and economic development among China, India, and Japan, a powerful country manager might be appointed to each. Elsewhere, a regional manager might be put in charge of a group of smaller countries. Transnational management remains appropriate for businesses with global customers, unitary brands, and products that require little or no adaptation around the world.

The Marketing Organization

How should marketing be organized within globalizing firms so as to maximize performance at all scales, from local to global? Among the key pieces are the role of the chief marketing officer (CMO), the organization of the global sales force, and the cultivation of marketing talent with the ability to act and think both globally and locally.

The Role of the CMO

Large multinationals typically have a global CMO and a CMO or equivalent high-ranking marketing executive in each of the major country markets. Smaller firms may have a CMO at headquarters and lower-ranked marketing staff under local management. But no matter how a multinational is organized, some degree of tension is inevitable in meshing global perspectives and experience with local marketing knowledge, formal reporting relationships with dotted-line relationships, and profit-and-loss responsibility with cost-center groups. Units with P&L responsibility tend to want to do things their own way, while functional or staff groups tend to want to enforce a common approach across the organization. Headquarters' influence over marketing decisions will run the gamut from informing, persuading, coordinating, and approving all the way to directing—depending on the issue and the relative power of each operating unit. The global CMO must be comfortable with using each mode and with the classic burden of having more responsibility than authority.

What should be clearly understood by management is that the CMO—or sometimes the CEO or strategic business unit (SBU) or division head—is ultimately responsible for the global brand name and product positioning. As former Tesco CEO, Terry Leahy, put it, "The bigger a brand becomes, the more sensitive it has to be to what its customers want. Its very size and fame make it more susceptible to consumer pressure. The knowledge that one slip can destroy a reputation that has been carefully nurtured over many years helps keep customers in the driving-seat."[17] The optimal marketing plan may call for local adaptations of the brand and positioning, but this should only occur with the approval of the global CMO.

The CMO may also be responsible for allocating an advertising budget across business units or countries, and prioritizing and accelerating the rollouts of new products. This person should have the clout to direct resources to places that offer the greatest growth opportunities—if necessary, at the expense of larger SBUs or countries—and to enforce the speedy rollout of new product launches around the world. A global CMO may control as much as 50 percent of the marketing budget in a company with a single global brand like Samsung, or as little as 5 percent in a highly decentralized multinational where the budget covers only corporate communications to investors.

The global CMO must ensure the rapid transfer of best practices and new product ideas. In this regard, clustering countries not by geographic region but by stage of brand and category development makes sense. Heineken, for example, plots countries on a four-quadrant map (see Figure 15), depending

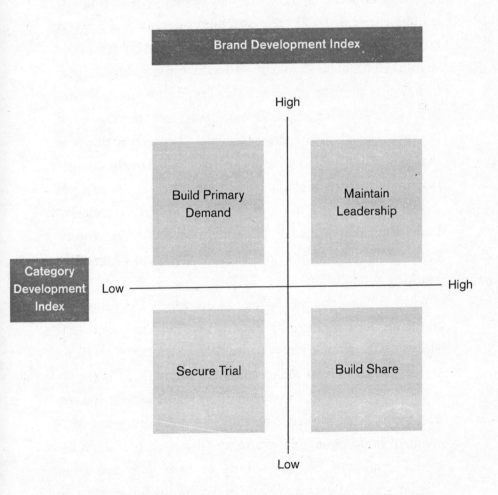

FIGURE 15. Focus of Marketing Depending on Level of Brand Development and Category Development in a Country

on whether they are high or low on a Category Development Index (beer consumption in liters per capita) versus Brand Development Index (Heineken brand market share). Marketing strategy objectives vary from one category to another. If there is little presence of the brand or the category, then the emphasis should be on securing trial. This may be done by securing distribution coverage and creating brand awareness. If there is little development of the category but the brand holds a major share, then the focus should be on developing primary demand, including educating consumers about product benefits. If category penetration is high but brand share is low, then the brand has to focus on building share by exploiting points of differentiation or identifying market niches overlooked by the competition. In mature markets with high category and brand development indices, the goal should be to maintain market leadership. Management will want to protect brand equity, grow through innovation, and engage in vigorous competitive blocking and tackling.

How far headquarters will go in allowing local autonomy in the implementation of marketing programs may appropriately vary from one country to another. Headquarters is likely to become more involved in countries where performance is poor or in smaller and newer markets where local managers require more assistance. Naturally, strong country management in large, profitable markets will have more organizational clout and be less willing to take direction from headquarters unless given a role in developing the strategy. In some cases, a national market may serve as a lead market for a region, where marketing programs are implemented first and then emulated if successful and modified if not.

Take the balancing act confronting Unilever. By the 1980s, the Anglo-Dutch conglomerate operated on every continent in a fairly decentralized fashion. Brand policies were largely set by the various brand managers in different geographies. This brought benefits of diversity and local responsiveness but problems of management control and a proliferation of brands with weak cross-national identity. In 2000, Unilever adopted a strategic initiative to winnow the number of brands from more than sixteen hundred down to about four hundred and to designate a smaller set of these as "master brands." For these global brands, Unilever instituted a dual management structure: one group for generating innovation and developing the brand, and one for controlling the business. The brand development head was put in charge of the strategic vision and global positioning for a brand or category and was usually located in the region where the brand was strongest. The brand building managers were geographically based and ran the execution of the strategy. This type of structure is well suited for building global brands. However, it can lead to conflicts over decision rights for such things as the resources allocated to a brand or the appropriate product portfolio within a particular country. Business growth was disappointing, and in 2005 Unilever concluded it needed to add on "a more active, aggressive, top-down approach to managing and building [its] portfolio," including better allocation of resources based on the alignment of brand strength and geographic strength.[18]

The Sales Organization

For the sales organization, the same issues of managing customer relationships discussed previously in Chapter 2 reappear on a larger scale. In transnational structures, business units tend to act like independent companies, often bumping into each other (and appearing uncoordinated) when approaching the same customers. In geographical structures, country units tend not to coordinate well in serving customers that are themselves multinational. In either case, global contracts signed at the customers' headquarters level must be fulfilled by local subsidiaries or local country units, which may receive no commission, and hence have weak incentives to cooperate. Furthermore, it is often impossible to negotiate globally standard prices and services when costs differ at the local level. But many multinationals have been pressed to do so, because global contracts that consolidate procurement inevitably advantage the buyer rather than the seller.

Likewise, the internal lack of coordination among multinational business customers may aggravate the global-local tension. Such firms may negotiate global or regional contracts that specify sole-source contracts for a particular product or service. But the success of these contracts depends on the success of multiple individual local transactions. If local employees of a multinational customer feel they have better relations with, or can obtain better value locally from, a different supplier—especially if they are evaluated on the local profit that they generate—they may well decide to ignore the global contract. Such behavior then undermines the sales volume assumptions on the basis of which the seller signed the global contract.

The organizational challenge of serving at the same time global customer accounts and country-specific national accounts thus mirrors the tension within a country between serving national accounts and smaller customers with limited geographical scope. Often, the result is a split sales force: Some salespeople—each with a distinct geographical territory—serve country or regional accounts, while a smaller team of global account managers deals with the very large customers that merit customized attention. Upper management must then be vigilant in ensuring coordination between the two sales forces.

Cultivating Marketing Talent

Attracting, retaining, and motivating top managers who think and act globally and locally is, of course, of prime importance for multinational companies. But the Chinese company Lenovo is one that may have overreached in its effort to forge a new kind of supranational East-meets-West culture. In 2005, Lenovo acquired IBM's personal computer business, giving it instant access to a global customer base and the number three position in global market share. English became the common corporate language, and the Chinese chairman moved to the United States, while the American CEO lived in Singapore. Research and development was split between China and North Carolina, and marketing was run out of Bangalore, India. Disparities in salary scales aggravated the problems of global coordination among management—while sales and profits in the home country were growing fast, Chinese executives were paid less than executives in the much less profitable U.S. market. Results disappointed and Acer of Taiwan took over the number three global share position, after Dell and Hewlett-Packard. Lenovo today emphasizes fast-growing Asian markets, and remains dominant, profitable, and respected in China. However, the supranational company, touted in Thomas L. Friedman's *The World Is Flat*, has all but disappeared.

Reckitt Benckiser, a consumer products company formed by a merger of UK and Dutch companies, has been much more successful in forging a workforce that sees both the global and the local pictures. Many global companies groom managers of different nationalities by rotating them through stints in various countries before returning them to a home country. However, Reckitt Benckiser cultivates people who view themselves as global citizens and don't expect to work in their country of origin. Every country has a mix of local employees and employees of many nationalities. The point is to hire people who are competitive, on the lookout for local opportunities, and willing to bring ideas forward. English is the official language and compensation rules apply equally to the top four hundred managers in all markets. There are uniform employment contracts, benefit and incentive plans, and salary ranges developed by global benchmarking; base pay is set near the industry median but performance-based bonuses are generous. The strategy appears to have paid off, in that, since

2005, Reckitt Benckiser's growth has outperformed competitors Procter & Gamble, Unilever, and Colgate—thanks in large part to a stream of successful new product introductions.[19]

In sum, companies as diverse as Reckitt Benckiser, Snapple, and Starbucks reveal that there is no one formula to determine how a company can establish a strong marketing presence outside its home market. Relevant considerations include the appropriate degree of customization in product and message for each place, suitable organizational structure, and available marketing talent. Succeeding locally and globally requires intimate knowledge of what local customers value (psychological space), how local customers live and navigate in their communities (physical space), and a clear understanding of alternative strategies for market expansion.

LIBRARY, UNIVERSITY OF CHESTER

CONCLUSION

Experts and observers are always quick to point to the changing business landscape and to predict the demise of old ways of thinking. Digital will displace physical; global will displace local; and new will displace old. But as we have seen, trends are rarely that black and white, and the movement toward one does not always mean the demise of the other.

Marketers face a complex landscape in which no customer can be purely global or purely local in outlook, and no customer can be purely physical or purely virtual in the way he or she buys. At the same time, increased access to the common pool of ideas, products, and services does not mean we all want the same things. Each of us is a unique mix of attitudes and opinions. In some cases, we see ourselves as global citizens connected by family, friends, or experience to far-flung places; at the same time we participate in the local communities where we live now and where we support local merchants and local products. In other cases, we may feel fiercely patriotic yet entirely open to buying the best-value brands we can find to meet our needs, regardless of their country of origin.

The price of not getting it right is high. In the world's most populous and fast growing consumer market, Best Buy closed all of its nine eponymous stores in China in 2011, just a few years after they had opened. Apparently, the American-style store did not meet the needs of Chinese consumers and could not match Chinese competitors. Home Depot closed all its Beijing stores, though it retained a foothold in second- or third-tier cities where overhead costs are lower. In 2006, the world's number one retailer, Walmart, left Germany and South Korea after disappointing results. For years, Walmart has lagged behind Carrefour in China and still has only a relatively few joint-venture stores there. Carrefour was considered to be superior at local adaptation.[1]

The forces of globalization have not yet come close to rendering place irrelevant. Nation-states remain the organizing structure for the world's population. Modern communications may enable individuals to build and join virtual communities that cross borders, but we are much more likely to use those resources to connect with our neighbor next door than a person on the other side of the world. Even those who are most global spend the bulk of their time within a small geographical area. The sense of place that comes with being part of a community—not the global village but the local village—remains an important part of our psyche, and, its continuity, a source of comfort and well-being.

Our place-based instincts remain more local than global. The more interconnected the world becomes, the more many of us wish to emphasize the local over the global. Such trends offer opportunities for marketers large and small. There are minimal barriers to market entry at the local level and an eagerness among many consumers to give local suppliers a chance. Anyone with a differentiated idea can set out a market stall. As for global marketers, they can capitalize on global efficiencies of scale and scope while customizing their offerings to meet the varying preferences of consumers living in one neighborhood versus another, in cities versus the countryside, in developed countries versus emerging economies, and on one continent versus another. At all levels, place still matters.

ACKNOWLEDGMENTS

This book has its genesis in decades of business experience and scholarship. In this effort to connect the dots and pull together the many streams of practice and thought related to place and location, we are grateful to all those who went before us. In challenging current assumptions about the role of place and location in a world transformed by globalization and the Internet, we relished the provocative ideas of numerous commentators.

A number of colleagues and friends kindly agreed to read and comment on the manuscript at various stages of development. We are particularly grateful to John Deighton and Sunil Gupta for their insights and suggestions on improving the manuscript.

We especially thank Jacqueline Murphy for ushering this project through to fruition. We also thank Timothy Ogden and Laura Starita for their sound editorial advice.

At Harvard, Elaine Shaffer cheerfully provided much-needed assistance throughout the project.

At Portfolio / Penguin, Brooke Carey provided first-rate editorial guidance and sharpened our thinking on many points. We are grateful to her and to Jamie Jelly for all their efforts on behalf of the book.

Funding for the research underpinning this work was provided by the Harvard Business School Division of Research. We thank Dean Jay Light for his continuing support of the project.

NOTES

Introduction: The Persistence of Place

1. Deloitte LLP (2010), "Real Madrid Becomes the First Sports Team in the World to Generate €400m in Revenues as It Tops Deloitte Football Money League," Press Release, Sports Business Group, March 2. London, available at http://www.deloitte.com/view/en_GB/uk/industries/sportsbusinessgroup/press-release/d039400401a17210VgnVCM100000ba42f00aRCRD.htm.

2. Real Madrid (2010), *Annual Report 09 10*. Madrid, available at http://www.realmadrid.com/StaticFiles/RealMadrid/InformeAnual0910_Ingles/pdf/Revista.pdf.

3. E. Jerome McCarthy (1960), *Basic Marketing: A Managerial Approach*. Homewood, IL, Richard D. Irwin, Inc.

4. Francis Fukuyama (1992), *The End of History and the Last Man*. New York, Free Press; Samuel P. Huntington (1996), *The Clash of Civilizations and the Remaking of World Order*. New York, Simon & Schuster; Jagdish Bhagwati (2004), *In Defense of Globalization*. New York, Oxford University Press; Martin Wolf (2004), *Why Globalization Works*. New Haven, Yale

University Press; Thomas L. Friedman (2005), *The World Is Flat: A Brief History of the Twenty-first Century*. New York, Farrar, Straus and Giroux; Al Gore (2006), *An Inconvenient Truth: The Planetary Emergency of Global Warming and What We Can Do About It*. Emmaus, PA, Rodale Press; Nicholas Negroponte (2006), "One Laptop per Child," *The World in 2006*. Ed. Daniel Franklin. London, *Economist*: 132; Richard Florida (2008), *Who's Your City? How the Creative Economy Is Making Where to Live the Most Important Decision of Your Life*. New York, Basic Books; Harm De Blij (2009), *The Power of Place: Geography, Destiny, and Globalization's Rough Landscape*. New York, Oxford University Press; Robert D. Kaplan (2009), "The Revenge of Geography," *Foreign Policy* (172) May/June: 96–105.

5. John A. Quelch and Kerry Herman (2008), "McDonald's," Case no. 9-508-025, April 3. Boston, Harvard Business School Publishing.

6. John A. Quelch and Katherine E. Jocz (2010), "Google in China (A)," Case no. 9-510-071, April 22. Boston, Harvard Business School Publishing.

7. Theodore Levitt (1983), "The Globalization of Markets," *Harvard Business Review*, 61(4) May/June: 92–102.

8. Nielsen Company (2010), "U.S. Ad Spend Falls Nine Percent in 2009, Nielsen Says," Nielsenwire, February 24. New York, available at http://blog.nielsen.com/nielsenwire.

9. Television Bureau of Advertising (2010), "Historical Cross-Media Ad Expenditures," Research Central-Ad Revenue Track. New York, available at http://www.tvb.org/nav/build _frameset.aspx.

10. Joel Garreau (1981), *The Nine Nations of North America*. Boston, Houghton Mifflin.

11. Bob Davis (2010), "As Global Economy Shifts, Companies Rethink, Retool," *The Wall Street Journal*, November 8: A1.

12. Hillary Rodham Clinton (1996), *It Takes a Village: And Other Lessons Children Teach Us*. New York, Simon & Schuster, 12.

13. John A. Quelch and Katherine E. Jocz (2008), *Greater Good: How Good Marketing Makes for Better Democracy*. Boston, Harvard Business Press.

14. Douglas B. Holt, et al. (2004), "How Global Brands Compete," *Harvard Business Review*, 82(9) September: 68–74.

15. Joel Kotkin (2009), "There's No Place Like Home; Fewer Americans Are Relocating Than at Any Time Since 1962," *Newsweek*, October 19: 42.

16. See Alex Taylor, III (2010), "How Toyota Lost Its Way," *Fortune* 162(2), July 26: 108–118.

17. Emma Jacobs (2010), "20 Questions: Sir David Tang, Entrepreneur," *Financial Times*, September 24: 14.

Chapter 1: Managing Psychological Place

1. Lee Cuba and David M. Hummon (1993), "A Place to Call Home: Identification with Dwelling, Community, and Region," *The Sociological Quarterly*, 34(1) Spring: 111–131.

2. Irwin Altman and Setha M. Low (1992), "Place Attachment: A Conceptual Inquiry," *Place Attachment*. Eds. Irwin Altman and Setha M. Low. New York, Plenum Press, 1–12.

3. Bart Bronnenberg, et al. (2010), "The Evolution of Brand Preferences," Working Paper, August 2. Chicago, University

of Chicago, Booth School of Business, available at http://faculty.chicagobooth.edu/matthew.gentzkow/papers.html.

4. World Public Opinion.org (2009) "People Who Know Foreigners or Travel More Likely to See Themselves as Global Citizens: Global Survey," May 18. Washington, DC, The Program on International Policy Attitudes, University of Maryland, available at www.worldpublicopinion.org/incl/printable_version.php?pnt=608.

5. Scott P. Johnson (2003), "The Nature of Cognitive Development," *Trends in Cognitive Sciences*, 7(3) March: 102–104.

6. Robert Sommer (1969), *Personal Space: The Behavioral Basis of Design*. Englewood Cliffs, NJ, Prentice-Hall.

7. Paul Shepard (1973), *The Tender Carnivore and the Sacred Game*. New York, Scribner.

8. Andrew J. Weigert (1981), *Sociology of Everyday Life*. New York, Longman.

9. Robert B. Riley (1992), "Attachment to the Ordinary Landscape," *Place Attachment*. Eds. Irwin Altman and Setha M. Low. New York, Plenum Press, 13–35.

10. Harold M. Proshansky, et al. (1983), "Place-Identity: Physical World Socialization of the Self," *Journal of Environmental Psychology*, 3(1) March–December: 57–83.; Edward T. Hall (1966), *The Hidden Dimension*. Garden City, NY, Doubleday.

11. Roger G. Barker (1954), *Midwest and Its Children: The Psychological Ecology of an American Town*. Evanston, IL, Row, Peterson; Roger G. Barker (1978), *Habitats, Environments, and Human Behavior*. San Francisco, Jossey-Bass.

12. Garreau, *The Nine Nations of North America*. Map available at http://www.garreau.com/main.cfm?action=book&id=3.

13. Patrick Chovanec (2009), "The Nine Nations of China," *The Atlantic*, November, available at http://www.theatlantic.com/magazine/archive/2009/11/the-nine-nations-of-china/7769/.

14. Claritas (2009), "Claritas Cartographics: Maps That Lead to Profitable Prospects," accessed at http://www.claritas.com/target-marketing/market-research-services/marketing-data/demographic-maps.jsp, on July 14, 2009.

15. Claritas (2008), "PRIZM NE Lifestyle Segmentation System," Brochure. San Diego, Nielsen Claritas.

16. U.S. Census Bureau (2009), "Geographical Mobility: 2009," May 10. Washington, DC, U.S. Department of Commerce, available at http://www.census.gov/population/www/socdemo/migrate/cps2009.html.

17. Andy Pike (2008), "Brand and Branding Geographies," *Geography Compass*, 3(1) December 12: 190–213.

18. Peeter W.J. Verlegh and J.B. Steenkamp (1999), "A Review and Meta-Analysis of Country-of-Origin Research," *Journal of Economic Psychology*, 20: 521–546.

19. As the leading marketing textbook defines it, "Positioning is the act of designing a company's offering and image to occupy a distinctive place in the minds of the target market...." Philip Kotler and Kevin Lane Keller (2011), *Marketing Management*. Upper Saddle River, NJ, Pearson Prentice Hall, 14th edition.

20. Al Ries and Jack Trout (1986), *Positioning: The Battle for Your Mind*. New York, Warner Books.

21. Lawrence E. Williams and John J. Bargh (2008), "Experiencing Physical Warmth Promotes Personal Warmth," *Science*, 322 October 24: 606–607.

22. Deborah Roedder John, et al. (2006), "Brand Concept Maps: A Methodology for Identifying Brand Associations," *Journal of Marketing Research*, 43(4) November: 549–563.

23. Gerald Zaltman and Robin H. Coulter (1995), "Seeing the Voice of the Customer: Metaphor-Based Advertising Research," *Journal of Advertising Research*, 35(4) July/August: 35–51.

24. Gerald Zaltman (2003), *How Customers Think: Essential Insights into the Mind of the Market*. Boston, Harvard Business School Publishing.

Chapter 2: Managing Physical Place

1. Truman Capote (1994) [1958], *Breakfast at Tiffany's: A Short Novel and Three Stories*. New York, Modern Library, 38.

2. Jack Neff (2010), "Why Packaged-Goods Players Are Bullish on E-commerce," *Advertising Age*, November 17, available at http://adage.com/print?article_id=147159.

3. John O'Doherty (2010), "Tesco Overseas Growth Offsets Slow UK," *Financial Times*, October 5; John Quelch (2010), "Tesco PLC: Fresh & Easy in the United States," Case no. 9-511009, August 11. Boston, Harvard Business School Publishing.

4. Jerry Useen (2007), "Apple: America's Best Retailer," *Fortune*, March 19.

5. Ibid.

6. Paco Underhill (2006), "The Way We Buy," *Conference Board Review* 44(6), November/December: 65–66.

7. Jeffrey S. Larson, et al. (2005), "An Exploratory Look at Supermarket Shopping Paths," *International Journal of Research in Marketing*, 22(4) December: 395–414.

8. J. Jeffrey Inman and Russell S. Winer (1998), "Where the Rubber Meets the Road: A Model of In-Store Consumer Decision Making," Working Paper, no. 98–122. Cambridge, MA, Marketing Science Institute: 34.

9. J. Jeffrey Inman, et al. (1990), "Promotion Signal: Proxy for a Price Cut?," *Journal of Consumer Research*, 17(1) June: 74–81.

10. Stephanie Clifford (2010), "Attention Shoppers: No More Aisle 3, 4, 5 . . ." *New York Times*, November 10: A1.

11. Stephanie Clifford (2011), "Stuff Piled in the Aisle? It's There to Get You to Spend More," *New York Times*, April 8: A1.

12. See Ram Bezawada, et al. (2009), "Cross-Category Effects of Aisle and Display Placements: A Spatial Modeling Approach and Insights," *Journal of Marketing*, 73(3) May: 99–117.

13. John Jackson, et al. (2007), "Recipe for Success," *Outlook: The Online Journal of High-Performance Business*, (2) May: available at http://www.accenture.com/us-en/outlook/Pages/outlook-journal-2007-packaged-food-nonalcoholic-beverages-industry-report.aspx; Julie Gallagher (2010), "Soup: Campbell Soup Co.," *Supermarket News*, October 11: available at http://www.supermarketnews.com/Grocery_Center_Store_Brands/soup-campbell-soup-co/index.html.

14. Bill Martin (2010), "ShopperTrak Measures Apple iPad Launch Traffic," Blog, April 2. Chicago, ShopperTrak.

15. Matthew Eggl and Christopher Vollmer (2009), "Major Media in the Shopping Aisle," *Strategy + Business* (Special Issue) Autumn: 90–100.

16. Natalie Zmuda (2010), "Check-in Apps' Next Stop: Your Supermarket Aisle," *Advertising Age*, 81(41) November 15: 4.

17. Stephanie Rosenbloom (2010), "In Bid to Sway Sales, Cameras Track Shoppers," *New York Times*, March 20: A1.

18. Robert R. Updegraff (1916), *Obvious Adams: The Story of a Successful Businessman*. New York, Harper & Brothers.

19. Eric Siemers (2010), "Nike Veers from Large Niketown Format," *Portland Business Journal*, May 14: available at http://portland.bizjournals.com/portland/stories/2010/05/17/story9.html.

20. John A. Quelch and Katherine E. Jocz (2009), "How to Market in a Downturn," *Harvard Business Review*, April: 52–62.

21. Useen, "Apple: America's Best Retailer."

22. Apple Inc (2010), "10-K for Fiscal Year Ended September 25, 2010," Investor Relations, October 25. Cupertino, CA, available at https://www.apple.com/investor/.

23. Tony Hernandez and David J. Bennison (2000), "The Art and Science of Retail Location Decisions," *International Journal of Retail and Distribution*, 28(8): 357–371.

24. R. L. Davies (1970), "Variable Relationships in Central Place and Retail Potential Models," *Regional Studies*, 4(1): 49–61.

25. Louis P. Bucklin (1971), "Retail Gravity Models and Consumer Choice: A Theoretical and Empirical Critique," *Economic Geography*, 47(4) October: 489–497.

26. Hernandez and Bennison, "The Art and Science of Retail Location Decisions."

27. Anheuser-Busch Companies and InBev (2008), "InBev and Anheuser-Busch Agree to Combine, Creating the Global Leader in Beer with Budweiser as Its Flagship Brand," Press Release, July 14. Leuven, Belgium, and St. Louis, MO.

28. Grocery Manufacturers of America (2002), "Reducing Out-of-Stocks Will Put $6 Billion in Retail Sales into Play," Press Release, June 10. Washington, DC; Marshall Fisher and

Raman Ananth (2010), *The New Science of Retailing: How Analytics Are Transforming the Supply Chain and Improving Performance*. Boston, Harvard Business Press.

29. Grocery Manufacturers of America (2002), "Up to 75 Percent of Global Out-of-Stock Issues Must Be Corrected at Retail," Press Release, October 14. Washington, DC.

30. Grocery Manufacturers of America, "Reducing Out-of-Stocks."

31. Fisher and Ananth, *The New Science of Retailing*. In the same period, sales actually dropped by 10 percent for a control group of SKUs, for which no efforts were made to improve in-stock rates.

32. Grocery Manufacturers of America, "Reducing Out-of-Stocks."

33. IBM and A. T. Kearney (2004), "A Balanced Perspective, EPC/RFID Implementation in the CPG Industry," White Paper. Washington, DC, Grocery Manufacturers of America, available at http://www.gmabrands.com/publicpolicy/docs/White Paper.cfm?docid=1402.

34. Coca-Cola Great Britain (2009), "Coca-Cola Announces the Carbon Footprint of Some of Its Best Loved Brands," Press Release, March 9. London.

35. Lindsey Layton (2010), "Most Eggs Produced by a Few Firms; Safety Inspections Fall through Cracks as Industry Consolidates," *The Washington Post*, August 24: A1.

36. James Tenser (2006), "Anheuser-Busch Taps into Store-Level Performance," *CPGmatters*, November, available at http://www.cpgmatters.com/CM1106Anheuser-Busch.html?cpgcatnet.

37. Stephen Pritchard (2010), "Mobile Apps Making Real Difference in Many Sectors," *Financial Times*, February 16: SR 2.

38. Andris A. Zoltners and Sally E. Lorimer (2000), "Sales Territory Alignment: An Overlooked Productivity Tool," *Journal of Personal Selling and Sales Management*, XX(3) Summer: 139–150.

39. Andris A. Zoltners and Prabhakant Sinha (2005), "Sales Territory Design: Thirty Years of Modeling and Implementation," *Marketing Science*, 24(3) Summer: 313–331.

40. Noelle McElhatton (2010), "An Extra Shot of Marketing," *Marketing*, February 3: 16, London, Haymarket Group.

Chapter 3: Managing Virtual Place

1. Association of American Publishers (2011), "AAP Publishers Report Strong Growth in Year-to-Year, Year-End Book Sales," Press Release, February 16, available at http://www.publishers.org/press/24/.

2. John Hanke (2010), "Introducing Google Places," The Official Google Blog, April 20. Mountain View, CA, Google, available at http://googleblog.blogspot.com/2010/04/introducing-google-places.html.

3. Internet World Stats (2009), "World Internet Usage Statistics News and World Population Stats," available at http://www.internetworldstats.com; Zia Daniell Wigder (2009), "Global Online Population Forecast, 2008–2013," Research Report, July 21. Cambridge, MA, Forrester Research.

4. TNS (2008), "Digital World, Digital Life," Press Release, December 19, London, Kantar Group.

5. John Horrigan (2008), "The Internet and Consumer Choice: Online Americans Use Different Search and Purchase

Strategies for Different Goods," Report, Pew Internet & American Life Project, May 18. Washington, DC, Pew Research Center.

6. J.D. Power and Associates (2007), "As Automotive Manufacturers Shift Marketing Dollars Online, New-Vehicle Shoppers Follow," Press Release, October 25, available at http://www.jdpower.com/corporate/news/releases/pressrelease.aspx?ID=2007237.

7. Mary Madden (2006), "Internet Penetration and Impact," Report, Pew Internet & American Life Project, April 26. Washington, DC, Pew Research Center.

8. Henry Harteveldt (2010), "US Online Leisure Travel Forecast, 2009 to 2014: The Plateau Is in Sight," Report, January 25. Cambridge, MA, Forrester Research.

9. Neff, "Why Packaged-Goods Players are Bullish on E-commerce."

10. Chris Anderson (2004), "The Long Tail," *Wired* (12.10), October, available at http://www.wired.com/wired/archive/12.10/tail_pr.html.

11. Facebook definition of active user: http://www.facebook.com/press/info.php?factsheet.

12. Comscore data cited in Mary Meeker, et al. (2009), *Economy + Internet Trends.* 4th Annual Future of Media Conference, New York, Morgan Stanley, November 3.

13. Amanda Lenhart and Mary Madden (2007), "Social Networking Websites and Teens," Report, Pew Internet & American Life Project, January 7. Washington, DC, Pew Research Center.

14. Nicole B. Ellison, et al. (2007), "The Benefit of Facebook 'Friends': Social Capital and College Students' Use of Online

Social Network Sites," *Journal of Computer-Mediated Communication*, 12: 1143–1168.

15. Pete Warden (2010), "How to Split Up the U.S.," February, Pete-Search Web site, available at http://petewarden.typepad.com/searchbrowser/2010/02/how-to-split-up-the-us.html.

16. Nielsen Company (2009), "Global Advertising: Consumers Trust Friends and Virtual Strangers the Most," Nielsen Wire, July 7, available at http://blog.nielsen.com/nielsenwire/consumer/global-advertising-consumers-trust-real-friends-and-virtual-strangers-the-most/.

17. Horrigan, "The Internet and Consumer Choice."

18. John Horrigan (2009), "The Mobile Difference," Pew Internet & American Life Project, March 25. Washington, DC, Pew Research Center, 6.

19. Data from Douglas Anmuth, et al. (2010), "Barclays Capital Internet Data Book February 2010," Equity Research, February 19. New York, Barclays Capital. Note that eBay is not counted among the e-retailers.

20. Stephanie Clifford (2010), "The Web as a Store Window," *New York Times*, August 24: B1; Nordstrom (2011), "Nordstrom Reports Fourth Quarter and Fiscal Year 2010 Earnings," *Business Wire*, February 17, available at http://phx.corporate-ir.net/phoenix.zhtml?c=93295&p=irol-newsArticle&ID=1530255&highlight=.

21. Jie Zhang, et al. (2009), "Crafting Integrated Multichannel Retailing Strategies," Working Paper, no. 09–125, April. Boston, Harvard Business School.

22. Jeonghye Choi and David R. Bell (2009), "Preference Minorities and the Internet: Why Online Demand Is Greater in Areas

Where Target Consumers Are in the Minority," Working Paper. Philadelphia, University of Pennsylvania, Wharton School; Jeonghye Choi, et al. (2010), "Traditional and IS-Enabled Customer Acquisition for an Internet Retailer: Why New Buyer Acquisition Varies over Geographies and by Markets," Working Paper, February 15. Philadelphia, University of Pennsylvania, Wharton School.

23. Ali Hortacsu, et al. (2009), "The Geography of Trade in Online Transactions: Evidence from eBay and MercadoLibre," *American Economic Journal: Microeconomics*, 1(1) February: 53–74.

24. Frank Cooper, Senior Vice President and Chief Engagement Officer, Pepsico Beverages America (2011), in biography available at http://www.effie.org/judging/juries/2011grand/Cooper.

25. Nielsen Company, "Global Advertising."

26. Miguel Helft and Tanzina Vega (2010), "Seeing That Ad on Every Site? You're Right; It's Tracking You," *New York Times*, August 30: 1.

27. (2010) "'Act Now, Apologize Later': Will Users 'Friend' Facebook's Latest Intrusion on Privacy?," *Knowledge@Wharton*, May 12, available at http://knowledge.wharton.upenn.edu/article/2482.cfm.

28. Sean Silverthorne (2009), "Understanding Users of Social Networks," *Harvard Business School Working Knowledge*, September 14: 1–2.

29. Universal McCann (2007), "Anytime, Anyplace: Understanding the Connected Generation," UM Global Digital Insight—In-depth Study 002, available at http://universalmccann.bitecp.com/um_report_pttp_lr3.pdf.

30. Ibid.

31. World Bank (2009), "Information and Communications for Development 2009: Extending Reach and Increasing Impact," May 22. Washington, DC, World Bank.

32. Meeker, et al., *Economy + Internet Trends*.

33. Ibid.

34. Cited in Ibid.

35. Larry Chase (2009), "Mobile Marketing Trends: Interview with eMarketer's Noah Elkin," Marketing Viewpoints by Larry Chase and Company, available at http://www.wdfm.com/marketing-viewpoints/noah-elkin-interview.php.

36. JiWire (2010), "Mobile Audience Insights Report Q1 2010," May. San Francisco.

37. JiWire (2010), "Mobile Audience Insights Report Q2 2010," August. San Francisco.

38. TNS (2008), "New Future in Store: How Will Shopping Change between Now and 2015?," Research Report, May. London, WPP, available at http://www.wpp.com/wpp/marketing/marketresearch/new-future-in-store. Countries surveyed were Canada, China, France, Germany, Japan, Spain, United Kingdom, and United States.

39. Andrei Hagiu and Bruno Jullien (2009), "Why Are Web Sites So Confusing?," *Harvard Business School Working Knowledge*, October 19, available at http://hbswk.hbs.edu/item/6303.html.

40. Henry Harteveldt and Elizabeth Stark (2010), "The Booking-Baffled Traveler," Report, April 23. Cambridge, MA, Forrester Research.

41. Zia Daniell Wigder (2009), "Global Online Population Forecast, 2008 to 2013," Research Report, July 21. Cambridge, MA, Forrester Research.

42. Ibid.

43. Douglas Anmuth, et al. (2010), "Barclays Capital Internet Data Book February 2010," Equity Research, February 19. New York, Barclays Capital: 30.

44. Gartner Inc. (2010), "Gartner Highlights Key Predictions for IT Organizations and Users in 2010 and Beyond," Press Release, January 13. Stamford, CT.

45. ABIresearch (2009), "Entry-Level Mobile Phone Markets to Enjoy 24% Annual Growth through 2014," Press Release, July 16. New York, available at http://www.abiresearch.com/press/1455.

46. Associated Press (2010), "EBay's Profit Rises 23 Percent on Pay-Pal Growth," *Moneynews*, October 21, available at http://www.moneynews.com/PrintTemplate?nodeid=374418.

47. Glenn Ellison and Sarah F. Ellison (2006), "Internet Retail Demand: Taxes, Geography, and Online-Offline Competition," Working Paper, no. 06–14, Department of Economics, April 28. Cambridge, Massachusetts Institute of Technology.

48. Jaeyeon Woo and Patrick McGroarty (2010), "Google Mapping Worries Spread—South Korean Police Raid Internet Firm's Offices; German Officials Criticize Street View Review Plan," *Wall Street Journal*, August 11: B4.

Chapter 4: Marketing Geographic Place

1. Harvard Business Review (2010), January/February issue: 4, 7, 11, 25, 43.

2. John Tagliabue (2010), "Switzerland, Beloved Bollywood Extra, Draws Indians," *New York Times*, July 12: A6.

3. Liz Alderman (2010), "Much Fiscal Pain in Ireland, But Low Corporate Taxes Go Untouched," *New York Times*, November 26: 1.

4. Michael Sasso (2007), "Retiree Flow to Florida Slows," *Tampa Tribune*, December 20, available at http://www2.tbo.com/news/south-shore/2007/dec/20/na-pipeline-of-seniors-to-florida-slows-ar-176826/.

5. Verlegh and Steenkamp, "A Review and Meta-Analysis of Country-of-Origin Research."

6. U.S. Department of Commerce (2010), "Key Facts about International Travel and Tourism," July. Washington, DC, available at http://tinet.ita.doc.gov; U.S. State Department (2010), "President Obama Signs Travel Promotion Act—New Law Seeks to Promote United States as International Travel Destination," State Department Press Release, March 5. Washington, DC.

7. Florida, "Who's Your City? How the Creative Economy Is Making Where to Live the Most Important Decision of Your Life."

8. Rana Faroohar (2010), "The Best Countries in the World," *Newsweek* 156(9), August 30: 30.

9. Institute for Strategy and Competitiveness (2010), "Cluster and Cluster Development," Web page. Cambridge, MA, Harvard Business School, available at http://www.isc.hbs.edu/econ-clusters.htm.

10. Diana Farrell (2004), "The Case for Globalization: The Results of McKinsey's Latest Study of the Pros and Cons of Emerging Market Foreign Investment," *The International Economy*, 18(1) January 1: 52.

11. (2005) "New Zealand changes investor immigration scheme," June 16, workpermit.com, available at http://www.workpermit .com/news/2005_06_16/australia/nz_changes_investor.htm.

12. Edward L. Glaeser (2007), "Can Buffalo Ever Come Back?," *City Journal* Autumn; Edward L. Glaeser (2010), "No Man Is an Island, Updated," *New York Times*, November 2, available at http://economix.blogs.nytimes.com/2010/11/02/no-man -is-an-island-updated/.

13. L. Finch (2010), "Fresh Farm Holiday Turkeys Gobbled Up," *Boston Globe*, November 23: 3.

14. American Express (2010), "Small Business Saturday (SM) Firmly Plants Its Roots between Black Friday and Cyber Monday," Press Release, December 2. New York.

15. For an interesting classification of the relationships between places and brands, see Cristina Mateo and Gildo Seisdedos (2008), "Different Branding Strategies from the Use of the Territory of Origin by Commercial Brands: The Brand-Territory Matrix," Working Paper. Madrid, IE Business School, available at http://bestplaceinstytut.org/www/wp-content/ uploads/2010/09/BrandterritoryMatrix.pdf.

16. IBM (2010), "Smarter Cities Challenge," available at https:// smartercitieschallenge.org/.

17. Pew Research Center (2008), "Global Public Opinion in the Bush Years," The Pew Global Attitudes Project, December 18. Washington, DC, available at www.pewglobal.org.

18. (2007) "View of US's Global Role 'Worse'," BBC News, January 23, available at http://news.bbc.co.uk/2/hi/americas/6286755 .stm.

19. Pew Research Center, "Global Public Opinion."

20. Globescan (2009), "Views of China and Russia Decline in Global Poll," *BBC World Service Poll*, February 6, available at www.globescan/news_archives/bbccntryview09/.

21. World Public Opinion.org (2009), "Obama Rockets to Top of Poll on Global Leaders; Putin and Ahmadinejad Receive Lowest Marks," June 29. Washington, DC, Program on International Policy Attitudes, University of Maryland, available at www.worldpublicopinion.org/incl/printable_version .php?pnt=618.

22. Norimitsu Onishi (2011), "U.S. Updates the Brand It Promotes in Indonesia," *New York Times*, March 6: A6.

Chapter 5: Marketing Locally and Globally

1. Levitt, "The Globalization of Markets": 94.

2. Previously both Coca-Cola and Pepsi licensed Soviet state bottling companies to produce and sell soft drinks.

3. Bart Bronnenberg, et al. (2007), "Consumer Packaged Goods in the United States: National Brands, Local Branding," *Journal of Marketing Research*, 44(1) February: 4–13; Bart Bronnenberg, et al. (2009), "Brand History, Geography, and the Persistence of Brand Shares," *Journal of Political Economy*, 117(1) February: 87–115.

4. Richard H. K. Vietor (2007), *How Countries Compete: Strategy, Structure, and Government in the Global Economy*. Boston, Harvard Business School Press.

5. Narin Sihavong and Erik Surono (2010), "Shiseido Company, Ltd.: Facing Global Competition," *Global Marketing Management*. Eds. Masaaki Kotabe and Kristiaan Helsen. New York, Wiley: 667–674.

6. Company documents in private communication with first author.

7. Before Southwest began service, competitors persuaded Congress to restrict operations to Texas. Later, as the entire industry was being deregulated, competitors persuaded Congress to pass the Wright Amendment, which prohibited through-passenger service from Love Field to any state except those contiguous to Texas (Congress finally eased the measures in 2006, with the law scheduled to expire in 2014).

8. J. Thadamalla, et al. (2008), "China's Automaker Chery's Global Expansion: Can It Race Past the 'Made in China' Image?," Case no. 308-398-1. Cranfield University, UK, European Case Clearing House.

9. Holt, et al., "How Global Brands Compete."

10. Boston Consulting Group (2008), "Foreign or Local Brands in China? Rationalism Trumps Nationalism," Focus series, June. Boston: 12.

11. E.J. Schultz (2010), "SABMiller Thinks Globally, But Gets 'Intimate' Locally," *Advertising Age*, October 4: 1.

12. (2007) "Brand Managers' High-Wire Act: Going Global and Staying Local," *Knowledge@Wharton*, October 31, available at http://knowledge.wharton.upenn.edu/article.cfm?articleid =1835.

13. World Business Council for Sustainable Development (2008), "Sustainable Consumption Facts and Trends: From a Business Perspective," Business Role Focus Area, November. Geneva, Switzerland.

14. Henkel (2010), "Sustainability Report 2009 Published; Strong Sustainability Performance," Press Release, February 25. Dusseldorf.

15. Levitt, "The Globalization of Markets."
16. Christopher A. Bartlett and Sumantra Ghoshal (1992), "What Is a Global Manager?," *Harvard Business Review*, 70(5) September/October: 124–132.
17. Terry Leahy (2006), "A Picture of People Power," *The World in 2006*. Ed. Daniel Franklin. London, *The Economist*: 90.
18. Patrick Cescau and Richard Rivers (2007), "Unilever's Growth Strategy," Unilever Investor Seminar, March 13. London, Unilever, available at www.unilever.com/.../ir _1.2_growth_strategy_rivers_speech_tcm13-86705.pdf.
19. Bart Becht (2010), "Building a Company without Borders," *Harvard Business Review*, April: 103–106.

Conclusion

1. Gary Gereffi and Ryab Ong (2007), "Wal-Mart in China: Can the World's Largest Retailer Succeed in the World's Most Populous Market?," *Harvard Asia-Pacific Review*, 9(1) Winter: 46–49.

INDEX